eight
twenty
eight

eight
twenty
eight

when love didn't give up

Ian & Larissa Murphy

B&H
PUBLISHING GROUP

NASHVILLE, TENNESSEE

978-1-4336-8182-0

Published by B&H Publishing Group
Nashville, Tennessee

Dewey Decimal Classification: 306.872
Subject Heading: LOVE \ MARRIAGE \ MENTALLY
HANDICAPPED

2 3 4 5 6 7 8 • 18 17 16 15 14

dedication

We know that for those who love God
all things work together for good, for those
who are called according to his purpose.
Romans 8:28

Written for our dad and teacher, Steve Murphy, who has
gone before us and now knows that all of this is worth it.
8/28/60–10/8/09

With courage we write this, in hopes that we all move
forward together in loving God more than loving comfort.

prologue

October 9, 2006
From Steve Murphy, Ian's Dad
It's been remarkable to me how much Mary and I have been at peace through this difficult experience. The Lord's grace has been present, even while grief overcomes us at different points. I had to talk to the insurance people about the car today, and for some reason I was really emotional talking to him about taking away the car that Ian was driving. I can tell that Mary is overcome at points, too, but I can tell she's also at peace.

We really are in faith at this point for whatever God has, but like you we're praying for an extraordinary miracle for Ian. God gives life and sustains life. God breathed new life into me when He saved me and made me a new creature. It's nothing for Him to raise Ian up from this coma. Thank you for the faith you have exhibited for a miracle. It's humbling, and we're grateful for your prayers.

originally posted on prayforian.com

a note from Ian

I just want to say that I love Larissa. God gave me a great thing in her. Larissa is my brain for book-writing, because I don't remember the years after my accident. It would be hard trusting Larissa to write down our story if I didn't love her. But I do, so all is well.

My hope is that you walk away from this book with something to think about. Because I want God to use this to make us better people—and strengthen relationships.

Trust God. He's bigger than your story. He's bigger than ours.

one

I sank down into my nap, covering my tired feet in the white down comforter, aching from another high-heeled day. The cloud settled over and in between my toes, legs, waist, and body, as its goose feathers warmed my skin. My husband wasn't home yet, and I was intent on making full use of this half hour of quiet. I glanced toward the unopened mail, the dirty sheets on the chair, and the half-full cups on the table, but allowed my eyes to drift shut before dwelling on what else I should be doing. All I could think of was rest before I would be forced to swing my legs to the edge of the mattress and out from under my little cocoon of heat.

As tiredness overcame me, my mind slipped in and out of sleep, thoughts rattling around in my groggy head until I couldn't distinguish between dreams and reality. I started feeling like I didn't remember him anymore. I couldn't remember his smile. I couldn't hear what his laugh sounded like or picture the way he walked. I couldn't find that place in me anymore that knew him, the part of my mind that stored the tone of his voice and the way he grabbed his stomach when he laughed hard. The thoughts I counted on to keep me going, to keep me in love, had left without asking my permission first. I couldn't grasp them. They felt like they were stuck somewhere in the very back corners of my mind, too far tucked away. Perhaps they were fighting from deep underwater to reach the surface—those memories and sounds and smells that kept him close and warm in me—but something was keeping them submerged. A flashback of sitting together on his patio or a note from him singing on a voicemail would start to break through, but before I could feel and grab it, the memory would sink back in, away from me.

"Have I really forgotten him?" my semi-awake brain begged as I awaited his arrival. "Have we been this way for so long that all of his old words and sounds are gone, that my memory can't keep them locked inside anymore? Is this all I'll ever be able to remember of him? This? *This* Ian?"

Then . . . the familiar thud of the van door, scattering even *these* thoughts into thin air.

I hopped up, brushed sleep out of my eyes, and peered through the bathroom window. In a few minutes, he and his wheelchair would be clattering through the door.

"Hi, wifey!" he shouted from the mud room once he'd made his way inside, driven from behind by his youngest brother, Devon. Ian couldn't control the volume of his voice anymore, and sometimes his speech was hard to understand. But "wifey" was usually LOUD and clear. Rolling into the bedroom, he saw me and hugged me. "How was your day?" I asked.

"I don't remember. So it must've been good!"

A typical response—because his short-term memory left when his brain injury came in. As a result, I was the only one of the two of us who was able to carry the detailed memories of our marriage, or of our ten months of dating before his accident, or of anything that reminded us of what life had been like before September 30, 2006.

The day it all changed.

The date that continues to roll around every year, whether I want it to come or not.

In the quiet of night before the most recent September 30, I had snuggled up close to him, unloading my heavy heart.

"Ian, I'm so sad. I'm sad for your brain injury. I'm sad you've had to go through this."

"That's why I love you," he said. "It makes you sad because you care about me so much."

There are very few anniversaries that I like anymore—most particularly this one—and I don't want Ian to recognize that I'm keeping count. But for me, there's no erasing the memories of that horrible September 30.

The most unwelcome anniversary of all.

two

We met in the spring of 2005, under a chance meeting between friends. I had spent the previous semester living in Australia as an eighteen-year-old American, a then-virgin to the clattering life of bars and clubs. Soon they and I had become regular friends, and most of the settings for my stories from that semester occurred inside their walls or spewed out on their sidewalks.

I had journaled my way through those three months, and it was clear from beginning to end that something was shifting in my heart, giving in. Darkness and emptiness had taken up root and grown wildly off the nectar of shot glasses and boxed wine. The nighttime had turned me into an angry young woman, the alcohol settling in and fogging my thought processes. The thick, tall sketchbook my sister had given me groaned with late-night words as each sentence I scribbled onto the paper recorded my sadness—and confusion—which all sort of crystallized around one question coming from my new friend Tracey while we sat on a Contiki tour bus, riding through the snow-capped mountains and green fields of New Zealand during the last month of our semester.

"You know that when you die, you'll go to heaven, right?" We were filling out paperwork to choose which adventure we'd undertake when we arrived in Christchurch. I committed myself to skydiving, and hours later would be gasping for breath as I somersaulted tandem out of the puddle-hopper plane. Thus the springboard for her question, I guess.

I hesitated.

"I don't know," I said, a first-time confession.

That moment, and Tracey's simple question, propelled itself backwards through months of bad decisions and guilt. It was an uncomfortable question to me. "When you die, you'll go to heaven, right?"

The only thing I knew for sure was that I was afraid of going to hell.

Meanwhile, across several continents and oceans, Ian was finishing up the same third semester of college as me. He was living at home with his parents and studying communications media, which also happened to be my major. We had different reasons for choosing it, though. I liked the low requirements for math courses. Ian actually wanted to use his degree to make films with his best friend David. They'd been making movies since they were little boy neighbors on Grandview Avenue—such as "Little Town," where their characters Max and Clubbert are really mean to a boy named Casey, who then gets hit by a car and whose ghost haunts them throughout the rest of the film. Complex and creative.

Since we were both communications majors, we ended up working at the campus TV station, which is where I first saw Ian, the semester I returned from Australia. A few passing interactions, a handful of words here and there, a quick hello. I didn't think much more about him.

But one night we ended up in the same apartment, a place the renters had coined "The Future." It was the first time we had talked together, more than a passing greeting, as we sat around the floor and on the couches. People were playing video games, and then someone put on some music. I watched as the boys turned into rag dolls, pulling their bodies into contortions and squirms. Someone with a camera froze the moment into a shot of Ian in his blue-striped dress shirt and crew cut, his hand reaching up to his head, his lips curled to wrap around a smile. A memory of a time that was simply easy.

I liked talking to Ian, but he still hadn't taken up residence in my thought patterns yet. It was only as we neared the end of the school year that I realized, through those same mutual friends, that we would probably be seeing more of each other. I was staying back to take a three-week summer class. And Ian, as well as friends Jimmy and Maelys, were all sticking around for the summer. All three of them were "townies" who hadn't strayed far from home for college, and I was staying on Fisher Avenue, just a few houses away from Maelys.

It turned into a summer that should never end. I wanted to just keep waking up to it the same way for years. It was a summer that memory tells me was sunnier than the ones today, despite being just as captive—then as now—to the rainy effects of Lake Erie.

Every night, the four of us found ourselves on adventures, sometimes with blankets to lay on the college football field or looking at the stars through the car windows, the girls in the back with our faces glued to the cold glass as Jimmy drove us in his green Explorer past the smokestacks of the power plant.

"They're just so big!" squealed Maelys through the window, her eyes following the thick smoke billowing into the sky as summer night greeted her cheeks. We erupted with laughter at her childlike excitement because we didn't need to be grown-ups yet. We didn't need to hold back or hold in because we were still young and still looking into an invincible future. I was seeing God in these friendships, enjoying the innocence of late-night trips to Dean's Diner. Everything ahead of me looked safe. The God that I was getting to know was gentle and patient.

"If you had to send someone into space on a rocket ship to never return back to earth, who would it be?" Jimmy asked from the driver's seat.

"Rob Thomas," said Ian without missing a beat, as if he would've *always* picked Rob Thomas, and everybody knew it.

"If you could live anywhere in the world, where would you pick?" Jimmy asked.

"Virginia, on a lake," Ian said.

I sat in the back seat, smiling to myself, wondering if this was a small coincidence. I had always wanted to live in Virginia, as well, on a lake. This was before I knew about the two weeks Ian spent there with his family every year.

"I don't know where I would pick," I said shyly, not wanting to sound like a copycat or a freaky stalker. I found out later that Ian had been hounded by several of those crush stalkers in his high school and college years, so his radar would've been up. I was glad I kept myself vague.

But more than the lighthearted, carefree fun of summer, something was shifting in my heart toward God, a desire I hadn't known since my high school days or even earlier. Things that I had known in my head were starting to take root in my heart.

For example, Ian invited my roommate and I to a class that was meant to explore Christianity, taking on the big questions and showing everyone how the Bible answers them. The classes were free, and they fed us before the discussions, which meant that a poor college student needed a solid excuse not to go. I usually sat near Tonya, who eventually became my college mom. And somewhere between the conversation and the sandwiches, the truth of Jesus and His accomplishment on the cross infused into my bloodstream. Faith came alive in me, and I was able to look at the world in a completely different way.

I became flesh. And I became God's.

And it was then that He switched my fate from hell to heaven.

Ian, on the other hand, had already been walking with God for a few years. He had walked up to his dad at youth camp and said he wanted Jesus in his life. Yet he struggled for years after that moment, knowing what he should be doing—knowing that what Jesus had already done was enough—but not always knowing how to sin less often, how to respond by pursuing holiness.

So we were both still messy, Ian and I—with misunderstandings and misgivings and no idea what years of faith would do for us. But God was there, using His masterful hand to draw us into Him.

And I sensed, however slowly, God was drawing us closer to each other.

"Keys!" I hear a coarse voice coming from the den. "Broad! Birch! Bring!"

He's practicing his speech, because those beginning sounds are hard to say, especially when a brain is as tired as Ian's. He and Devon are working, working, working, just like he's been doing for the past six years. To get better.

His voice wasn't always like this. Before his accident, Ian sang all the time, and loudly. He sang about free-falling with Tom Petty, his long-haired head slung out the driver's side car window. He sang on our pastor's memory verse albums. He sang in Knucklehead, his band with friends Mark, David, and Justin. He sang five-minute voicemails to me, obnoxiously romantic songs that would later trap me in memories while I sat on the hard, cold, ICU hallway floor.

Now, though, his voice is rough and the breathing uncalculated. When he sings Tom Petty, his voice doesn't follow the melody. But it makes me laugh harder than ever. Because I'm pretty sure, despite it all, my husband is somehow happier than ever.

Even though Ian had a great voice and sly smile, it took a while for me to think of him as more than just a friend. "Ian's really hot," I had said to Maelys that summer, before he and I were dating, "but I'm not really attracted to him."

"Me either," she said, both of us confused as we walked down the street behind the boys. Yet it just didn't add up to us. He had a Tom Cruise face and an irresistible smile.

I had a hunch that maybe my ambivalence was because of how much he annoyed me. Because even though we'd become friends, it was a love/hate relationship from my end. A little on his too. I mean, sure, he was funny. Smart. Magnetic. He was all of those. But unfortunately, he was also incredibly annoying. Things that were common sense to me—a simple country girl raised on basic, practical chivalry and old-fashioned manliness—he just didn't do them.

"You'd make the worst boyfriend in the world," I told him as we stepped away from the lazy Susan bagging thing at Walmart. I was buying groceries to make him lasagna, and as I checked out, he just stood by and watched me grab the somewhat heavy bags. *My dad would never have just stood there*, I thought.

Then there were the times when Ian felt like the rules didn't apply to him, at least not *my* rules, and at least not from my perspective. Like carrying full mugs of coffee into department stores. Didn't he realize he could spill his drink all over the merchandise, and then we'd have a crisis on our hands? Or like giving five dollars less in gas money than everyone else on group road trips. Or like using only conditioner instead of shampoo for weeks because he liked how greasy it made his hair look. Or like not knowing how to adequately drive a stick shift, even though he said he did and then jerked us for four blocks to drop off a friend in a borrowed car.

Hopelessly devoted to my diaries since I was seven, I confessed often about Ian, dramatizing the feelings I was trying to hold captive. Even though my journal dramatically tells me that thoughts of Ian were "poisoning my mind," he was poisoning it with what would become some of the best memories of my life.

Sometimes he just lived in a different world. But it was a world that I needed.

It took us a few weeks of "fake dating" before actually making the commitment. We tried to be careful with our hearts, with our feelings, but we were just having so much fun. And then somewhere around the end of November, deep into our fall semester, Ian asked me, "Do you have any plans tomorrow night?" We were in the car on our way to pick up a friend and go bowling together. I told him, no, I didn't have plans. At first I didn't really think about what his question meant. We hung out so often, it didn't strike me as anything but ordinary.

Then I got it.

I realized he was asking me to "go on a date" with him, which meant that after many conversations about what our future should or could look like, he was ready not to be "fake dating" anymore. And because we'd had those hypothetical conversations, I knew he'd be dating me to see if he wanted to make me his wife.

I didn't know it then, but he had been talking with his parents about why he wanted to date me, asking if they felt like he was ready to pursue a relationship that could potentially lead to marriage. He told them I had a teachable heart and was willing to grow in my understanding of God—and he loved that. It refreshed him. He said I also wasn't afraid to challenge *him*. He liked that too.

His dad said the fact that he was asking if he was ready to date me was a good indicator that he probably was.

And so, yes, he had their blessing.

We arrived at the bowling lanes that night—the night he had asked me to go to dinner the *next* night—and suddenly everything felt different. Looking at him felt different. Catching him glancing at me felt different. I couldn't have been more excited to be giving in to the feelings I had tried to hold inside, feelings I could now delve into because he also had them for me in return. I didn't know it at the time, but I was stepping into a universe of God's design that had been created for us at the cross, when Jesus stepped into death on our behalf and created the perfect way to love. Our love could never be as perfect as His, of course, but as children of God we were able to receive love vertically from Him that we could learn how to extend to each other. We were on the brink of understanding the strength that love can inspire in us and the extent to which it holds us. I couldn't have predicted it, but through Ian and because of his decision to ask me to become more than just an extra in his life, I would inherit communion with Christ that would only be found through the gaping pause our love would soon come to know.

I wanted my parents to know this new love and to feel it with me. At first, when I asked them to come out and meet him, they thought he was just another college boyfriend. This wasn't the first time I had told them I'd found my future husband. Still, they traveled with my sister to my campus apartment for a weekend to meet Ian and test him against the family "man" standards. My mom told me later that she was skeptical about him, but then she saw him smile—that deep smile of his, the one that exposed his gums and gave a glimpse into the sweet man behind the sarcasm.

The moment she saw that smile, she knew why I was in love.

I began to see the hidden heart in my best friend—a side with a different tone of voice that said yes to just about anything I asked, simply because he was in love.

"I couldn't believe someone ever liked Ian enough to date him," his aunt Andrea joked years later as we were painting a bedroom at Ian's mom's house. But the reason it was hard for her to believe was because the outward Ian often only showed the humor, the wit, the sarcasm, not the heart. It took context to get to Ian's heart—and I loved that. It made me feel special, like he trusted me.

Andrea was one of three family members that Ian said *had* to like me. I don't know what the consequences were going to be if they didn't, but Ian told me on the way to Philadelphia for Easter that I'd be meeting many people that weekend, but only really needed to win over three: Aunt Andrea, as well as cousins Jessie and Sarah.

Jessie and Sarah were the girl cousins closest to Ian's age, and they were like sisters to him. I soon came to realize they loved him more than I ever could, because something special happens when you've had someone in your life for everything as far back as you can remember. Something happens on a vacation each year for two weeks, going to day camps at Silver Bay and kayaking on Lake Anna, disappearing from the family crowd for hours. They'd built years together on long wooden picnic tables at vacation houses and through watching old Hitchcock films on VHS for hours, Ian keeping a hilarious running dialogue of the films. They'd become best friends as they slept in Grandma's den, staying up late talking and laughing and sharing stories, then raiding the cupboards, hoping to discover a stash of salty potato chips.

Over the years of vacations and Christmases and Easters together, Sarah and Jessie made Ian gentler, probably unintentionally, simply because they gave him exposure to girls and feelings that he wouldn't have known otherwise. He felt comfortable enough to say whatever he felt to them.

But it was a gift that didn't translate so well to a girl who was your girlfriend, not just your cousin. Case in point:

"I could see your mustache from across the room," he said to me as we sat in my apartment, just returning from our campus ministry. Mortified, my eyes started to water. And just like that, I pelted him with bombs of estrogen and emotion, leaving him clueless to the dramatic, circular conversation that would ensue.

As he spoke, I imagined him back where he first saw it—the 'stache. Flirtatiously turning his head around to find me in the room, his long, brown hair trailing slightly behind him, he lays eyes on his beautiful girlfriend and starts to smile. But then, aghast, he sees not his young bride-to-hopefully-be, but instead a dastardly thick, black, long mustache that drapes and curls over her upper lip, like a fur stole looping around a delicate shoulder. Catching his eye, I give an equally flirtatious smile and nod, but he can only choke down repulsed horror in response. He then feels like he needs to say something, needs to tell me about this huge, hairy thing on my face, to spare and protect me from the deep scars of embarrassment and shame.

"Larissa, why are you crying about this? I could say this to my *cousins*," he said with a tenderly confused voice.

"But I'm not your cousin! I'm your girlfriend! And it's embarrassing!"

"I thought you'd want to know so you could do something about it."

"Couldn't you have said it differently than saying 'you could see it from across the entire room'?"

Then of course, as many well-intended man comments have the tendency to unbridle, the conversation spiraled further, as I brought up things that had nothing to do with Ian and yet felt perfectly relevant. Like that there was someone prettier than me in my English class that he might meet someday and decide he liked better.

He did his best to navigate my mess, but instead found himself in a Hitchcock parody on his three-mile ride home, replaying the conversation, trying to figure out how he could have prevented it—or at least how he could weave his mistake into a future screenplay.

He must've lain awake thinking about it that night, because he broke into my apartment through the waist-high kitchen window the next morning while I was at class.

Placing my favorite candy bars everywhere, he made his peace offering and I gladly accepted. In fact, the mustache conversation soon became one of our favorite and most hilarious memories, as soon as I could see Ian's attempt at love through it.

Laughter was familiar to us, like the time when I visited him for the day in Lancaster where he was doing his internship on the set of a feature film. We were walking around town after eating lunch at a pizza shop, when I suddenly squealed as a buggy rolled past us.

"Ian, was that a mannequin?"

He couldn't resist.

"Yeah, mannequins drive buggies in Lancaster."

"Wait, was that really a mannequin? His face looked like plastic and his cheekbones were perfect and he didn't move. That was definitely a mannequin."

I swirled through the possibilities and logistics—such as, how in the world did the mannequins know to stop at red lights? Somehow the whole thing made plausible sense in my head for too long, and Ian held a straight face for too long, and he added too many convincing facts to his case, keeping me hanging for too long. But when the spell finally broke, I ended up hitting him in the arm, laughing hysterically, and yelling at him for making me believe such deception.

There were also the constant debates over how to pronounce Eat'n Park, the restaurant at the intersection by his parents' house, the intersection we eventually lived above in our first rental house as a married couple.

"Larissa, you're supposed to actually pronounce the word 'eat'—with the 't' sound. Go ahead, say it."

"Eden Park," I demanded back, my country upbringing hiding the t's in the middle of words, like mitten, kitten, and mountains. It sounded fine to me, but foreign to him. We kept arguing, because it was fun, and it gave us something to do.

He tried to teach me the proper use of the word *touché*, something I'd never heard before he brought it up. I tried it out several times later. "No, that's not even close to how you're supposed to use it," he would say back between laughs.

He pitched T-shirt ideas to me that he stored in his idea books, like the shirt he wanted to make to celebrate Daylight Savings Time. "Daylight Savings Time: Turn Back the Clocks." Or the one he wanted to make about Davy Jones' backpack, which was somewhere within Davy's locker. Unfortunately the joke was lost on me, and I sat on the couch as he stood in front of the TV, his loafers shuffling on the carpet and his arms swinging out in front of him, perplexed that I didn't get it. He always used his arms and hands to talk, and I loved to follow his thick silver watch as it traveled up and down his wrist with the movements.

I loved him even more after we went swing dancing in Pittsburgh and then tried to show off our moves to his parents, moves where he lifted and twisted me. My mom had only recently convinced my dad to take dance lessons after twenty-five years of asking, and I wanted that for myself too. Unfortunately, Ian dropped me during the demonstration, and I rolled into belly laughter, my plastic hair clip broken into pieces on the ground, and his mom, Mary, worrying that I had been hurt.

Winning my heart over and over was a challenge he had looked forward to and spent a lot of time coordinating. He often used laughter as a sharp tool to get to my heart, when he wasn't using well-orchestrated, well-intended deceit.

He found out, for example, that I liked when he wore his steel-toed boots. They felt like a real man's shoe to me. They reminded me of my dad. My dad was raised on a farm and later sold farm equipment. He was the high schooler who drove and raced muscle cars. His nickname was Hammer because of the size of his biceps. He could do and fix anything. Until he went back to college at thirty for a degree in radiology, he was the dad who went to work in steel-toed boots and clothes made to get greasy.

Ian wasn't that. At all. Which I was okay with, even though he tried. But once he realized I liked him wearing those steel-toed boots, he wore them all the time. With sweatpants. With cut-off shorts. With jeans.

In another attempt to prove his manliness—to try keeping up with the man who'd raised me—he offered to fix my broken coffee table. I don't remember if it was actually fixed by the time he was done, but I do remember watching him come in my apartment door with his dad's tools, as if he knew what to do with them. I sat there watching him crouch down on his knees as he turned the coffee table on its side, assessing the damage and making up a way to fix it.

Somehow he found out I liked jazz music. I had always wanted to marry someone who liked jazz music, and so it soon became the sound track to our nights playing speed Scrabble or doing a crossword together on the couch, our feet resting on the precariously stabilized coffee table.

The furniture was standing, but I was falling.

———

Ian was dating me with the intention of marriage, and this intention was melting my young heart into little puddles. They were muddy puddles, filled with messiness and expectations and imperfections. But the images reflecting back up at me were ones that I had imagined since I was a little girl, because I was happy. He had chosen me.

He was wanting to learn to know me—and learn to know if he could know me his whole life. I couldn't understand in my head what it would be like to be a wife, to be *his* wife, someone who in so many ways was his opposite. Yet my heart knew that time away from him wouldn't do me good.

Time and sleep and school did their best to keep us apart, but we found ways.

He recommended that we start reading through the gospel of Matthew together. That took my heart a little bit more.

He encouraged me to start a small accountability and prayer group with a few girls. He wanted to help me grow stronger spiritually.

He took me to get a Christmas tree, cutting it down and getting it into the car and setting it up in the stand. He offered to take it out too, once the holidays were over, then dragged so many needles down the exterior hallway that we later got a letter from the landlord. What I didn't know was that his version of taking it out of my apartment meant sticking it in the front yard shrubs at his mom's house and not telling her, just waiting until she noticed.

On Valentine's Day, he left a series of lists around my apartment. They were top ten lists, like, ten reasons why I was good for his health, citing among them a growing six-pack from laughing with me so much.

He advocated for me when I was uncomfortable socially— a plain girl matched up alongside his huge personality and presence. But he also encouraged me to have confidence enough to defend myself when necessary so that someone couldn't take advantage.

He was proving good for me.

I turned twenty-one that March, the cold air reminiscent of my eighth birthday party back in 1993, when a blizzard in our mountains caused all my little girlfriends' parents to come take them home early. Winter was on top of us in March 2006 as well, but it felt warm inside knowing that Ian had planned something special for me. We sat opposite each other at the tiny breakfast table at 701 Café, a little place on the corner of Seventh and Philadelphia Street. It was tucked into the corner of a drugstore that sold my favorite greeting cards, and it had a small street-side window where passersby could pick up a coffee or one of the café's famous capitol rolls. Mary told me once that there used to be a Capitol Diner somewhere on Philadelphia Street that was known for the rolls. Somehow the secret recipe travelled up a block to the café, and the results sat behind the glass casing next to the checkout register, the clear glaze just begging. We shared birthday breakfast and watched the group of gray-haired men that looked like regulars as they walked to their table, wondering what it would feel like to be them.

We sunk into the apartment couch for hours that afternoon, enjoying my birthday present of several discs folded into the sleeves of a TV miniseries. The orchestration of the day showed that he knew me, and the words scribbled into my birthday card showed the simplicity of his heart . . . that he was simply glad I'd been born.

Ian was the kind of guy who would drive me home in my car when I was too tired to drive myself. That meant my Ford Focus would often sit in his parents' driveway overnight, which made me feel like I was special to him. I loved to be taken care of, because that's exactly how my dad had raised me. I wasn't coddled as a child or taught to be helpless, but I knew he'd be changing the oil in my car and taking it to get the tires checked. As Ian grew to know me, he started to realize that those things were important. He loved me through the little, and the big.

He also cried with me.

He cried when we talked about choices I had made before I knew him, before I loved him, before I knew how much those choices would hurt. We sat in his Mazda, a few months before it would die in the Honors College parking lot, green foam pouring out of the engine. We both cried on the maroon pleather back seats, each set of our legs folded up into pretzels against the backs of the driver and passenger seats. He held my hand, forgiveness wrestling through his heart. My tears dripped with guilt, watching my mistakes clatter against his expectations and the guards he had put in place for himself. I watched as his own tears ran out and forgiveness came, followed by the sweetness of mercy.

"One of the things I love the most about you is that I see Christ in you," he said to me. Our relationship as a Christian couple was coming to life before him, opening up on the sidewalks we roamed together, trickling out as his fingers rounded through mine. He would point out areas of sin in my life, and he encouraged me to do the same for him. More than words on the worn-out pages of his Bible, we were moving from stone to flesh, from lifeless clay to pottery, agreeing to wash away ourselves until the pure white shown through. We were challenging each other on our views and expectations of the future. The longed-for days ahead increasingly joined our conversations as we dated and fell into each other, longing even more to join our story lines together.

We were exploring our expected future with anticipation, as well as with naïveté. We loved strongly, but with bouts of fear and timidity. We loved without knowing what we would do with it or why we had been given it or if it would last as long as we hoped.

If we had known that our lives had already been given to each other . . . if we had seen on our first date at the old Train Station Restaurant that a simple interest would too soon be tested by a shunt and ventilator . . . if we had known the white station wagon that drove us on dates to see campus plays and go bowling would be slammed underneath the belly of an oncoming SUV . . .

If we had known, would we have kept going?

"She couldn't leave," Mary told a reporter a few years later. "She was already in too far."

I wanted to get married in the spring. After we graduated in December, I wanted to plan an outdoor wedding and start applying for jobs in D.C. Ian wanted to work with someone he had met on his summer internship. We wanted to have a city life. We wanted to start our twenty-second year as newlyweds. He wanted to buy me a ring, wanted to work two jobs to pay for it, and wanted to make me his wife.

We had *everything* we wanted.

And we couldn't want it fast enough.

"Why do you want to get married?" my parents asked us one Friday night as we sat opposite them on their blue davenport, home for my sister's wedding shower over a cool weekend in September.

We looked at each other, my twenty-one-year-old hand locked into his twenty-one-year-old hand that I claimed always suffocated my tiny, fragile fingers. We looked at my parents, married at eighteen and twenty, nervously hoping for their approval.

"Because we love each other," Ian said.

My dad didn't know it, but Ian had been hoping—if the right opportunity came along that weekend—to ask his permission to take my hand and to fill it with a ring. Maybe the next morning would be the proper time.

But as I left early to decorate the church sanctuary with tablecloths and wedding bell confetti for my sister's party, my dad took Lisa's fiancé and Ian into the barn and asked them to help move some bales of hay with him . . . *arbitrarily*, according to Ian. Just to pick them up and set them back down again. Or so it seemed.

Ian worked for just a few minutes before the nausea started flowing over him. Not wanting to look like a wimp but having a lifelong propensity toward vomiting easily, he leaned over and threw up next to the hay bales. Maybe this wasn't such a good time after all to make his marriage appeal.

Later, when the festivities should've been wrapping up, my dad and Kurt and Ian drove to the church to load up the Crock-Pots and the blue and tan bathroom towels and everything. Ian found me inside on the sparsely padded folding chairs that doubled as pews, and he told me the story. He'd been lying on the couch ever since, and my only response was to erupt in laughter.

Looking back, it was probably the nerves of a young boy asking a big question to a fairly unfamiliar man. It was the queasy feeling that told him maybe he wasn't ready, that maybe he needed to wait just a little while. He figured the next time he would get a chance to ask my dad would be at my sister's wedding that October—which wasn't that far away. So he held out hope.

———

"Good morning, husband," I utter as the Sunday fog finally clears just enough for words.

"Good morning, wifey."

"I'm making pancakes for our breakfast."

"That sounds perfect."

"If you'd let me quit my job, I'd make you pancakes every morning."

"Deal."

Looking at him, I smile with the weight of a hard-earned love. I call Devon in, who begins to help my husband sit up in bed, then transfers him to a shower chair, then pushes him into the bathroom.

This is year six, I think to myself as the second batch of pancakes starts to bubble on the cast iron skillet. And we have to keep going.

three

On Friday, September 29, 2006, Ian and I spent the evening with his Murphy grandparents, who were visiting from the east. We had dinner with them and the rest of Ian's siblings, and then sat catching up around the fireplace.

Ian asked me if I'd work with him the next day. He was headed an hour north to paint the walls inside a house that his dad's company had just purchased. Steve was working for a company that bought foreclosed houses, so both Ian and I were able to do contract work for them. I spent hours scrubbing disgusting, cruddy walls and toilets. My friend Jan often worked with me, and we would make up stories as the Magic Eraser dissolved underneath our wall scrubbing. We took rooms on the same floors as each other so our voices wouldn't get lost and so we wouldn't get creeped out in the dirty, dingy basements.

Ian did everything from painting to gardening to "trashing out" all the leftover items from the last owner. He took his job seriously, working hard to earn enough money for a ring. But he was still Ian, of course, even as an employee.

One time, for instance, as he and his brother Ben picked me up to go clean a house together, he got out of his car in a one-piece gray jumpsuit, the pant legs ending much too far above his ankles. He looked so dumb. But he made me laugh.

"Work tomorrow?" I answered. "No, I can't. I've got that wedding shower in the morning."

"Oh yeah. Well, I just wondered."

After a few hours, his grandparents left for the hotel and the boys scattered into the den for video games. Ian and I sat on the white and blue couch with the pullout bed in a now quiet room. I remember bits of our conversation. I was talking irrationally about my feelings on something. I remember Ian trying to talk me through it, but it was getting late, and I was past the point of making sense.

"You need to get home," he said, half laughing. "You just need to get some sleep." I loved that he knew me so well, that he wanted to take care of me.

After I left, he set off on foot to walk the ten minutes to David's house, wearing his green corduroy jacket. Adam, a childhood friend of Ian and David's, was in town along with another friend. They spent hours on the patio that night, enjoying conversation that comes when you've known someone a lifetime.

David offered to give Ian a ride home so he wouldn't have to walk back. Ian didn't take him up on his offer, though.

The next morning—Saturday, September 30—I sent Ian a text just to say I loved him. Then I was off with Jan, leaving early to go shopping for the wedding shower later. So I didn't particularly notice amid the car conversation that Ian hadn't sent a reply. After a few hours of shopping and rushing home not to be late to the party, Jan dropped me off at my house, and I ran upstairs to wrap our gifts. I sent another text. I remember standing next to my car several minutes later, ready to leave, looking at my phone. He still hadn't written back. It seemed strange to me. But I didn't spend much time thinking about it. He was probably just busy. Painting. Mowing. Something.

I had never been to Carolyn's house before, host of the shower. It was long and sprawling and perfect for parties. I would later hear stories, however, that told how the party perfection hid structural issues with the house that had plagued her and her husband for years. Underneath the bold Victorian patterned wallpaper and man cave covered with deer mounts was an uneven foundation that caused skewed door and wall joints. But because of Carolyn's ability to turn normal into hilarious, anyone who heard her horror stories couldn't help but laugh at the absurdity.

I walked in, unsure of myself because I didn't know many of the other women there. I timidly took a plate of food and tried hard to make conversation. I would be doing better if Ian were there with me. He was good at initiating conversation and filling in my awkward gaps. I liked people better when Ian was with me because small talk wasn't so scary.

Soon after everyone arrived, we shuffled into the living room near the fireplace—the same fireplace where they had once discovered another major flaw in the house. An entirely messed-up ventilation system had been allowing the flames just to shoot up through the walls, which made it a wonder that the house and the fireplace were still standing. But on this day, Jen (another friend—not Jan) was sitting on the couch, gifts for her new life at her feet. She had started dating Stephen a few months after Ian and I began seeing each other. He had proposed in Pittsburgh, along the river. She cleaned houses with me sometimes too, and she knew how much I loved Ian.

We prayed for Jen.

We started a worship song.

We sang with our eyes closed.

Then I felt a hand on my shoulder and a whisper in my left ear.

"Steve just called," Mary said. "Ian's been in an accident. He's in a Pittsburgh hospital. We need to leave."

With those words, life shifted. With those words, my role in Mary's life, in Ian's life, in my family's life, in everyone's life would take on a whole new identity. With those words, Ian was removed from his normal body and was given a new label—a label that would change everything.

I would give anything to take those words back, those breaths back, to shove them up into a tight ball, sealing them with tape and glue and cement to make sure they never opened back up.

But in that moment, those words caused the singing voices of the partygoers to warp in my head. My palms started to sweat. Fears instantly surfaced alongside fresh tears. My gut told me this wouldn't be small.

I mumbled something to Jan and said goodbye, as murmurs of the phone call Carolyn had received from Steve filtered quickly through the room. We hurried out the door. The song, the food, and the laughter didn't matter anymore. For the next few years they still wouldn't matter. Something was wrong, something was keeping Ian from getting in his car and driving back home to me, and we just needed to know.

I left my car with the women at the shower so Mary and I could stay together. My mom and sister Lisa were supposed to visit me that day. I called them to say they shouldn't come. I called to say that Ian had been in an accident. I called to say that I didn't know what else to say.

We pulled into the Murphy driveway fifteen minutes later, and Steve met us outside with his cell phone and red hoodie. Transferring us to his company Taurus, he replayed his conversation with the social worker, the kind of horrible call that jolts families without asking their permission first.

Someone had called the house while the three younger boys were in the den playing video games and Steve was in the bedroom. The person had started to leave a message, and by the tone of the voice on the machine, Ben thought something was wrong. Grabbing the receiver, he ran up to give the phone to his dad. That's when Steve met the social worker, who was the "someone" on the other end of the phone. Ian had been in an accident. He didn't tell Steve what kind of accident or where it had happened, but simply that Ian was in surgery in Pittsburgh.

The longest fifty miles ever were ahead of us, and the tissues next to me wound their way into my hands. We didn't say much. All my energy was focused on my tears and the new loneliness that was settling in. After all, the only reason I knew these two other people in the car was because I knew Ian, but he wasn't there with me, and he wasn't there to help me. I sat in the back, behind Mary's seat, trying to put one thought in front of the other, one scared thought behind the last. We were scared, but not frantic. At least Mary and Steve weren't. Not frantic. They were able to keep a steady calmness, a patient trust, even in a moment when most people would be coming apart at the seams. They weren't the kind to overreact prematurely.

But in the back seat, being pulled along on the fifty-mile drive that would soon become a daily commute, I feared for Ian's brain. "God, please don't let it be his brain. Anything but his beautiful brain," I pleaded.

I didn't know it then, but Mary's prayers echoed mine.

I remember seeing a billboard to my right, through the window that watched me as I cried. According to the pictures of the surgeons on those billboards, Ian's brain would be okay (if the problem *was* his brain), because these doctors, it said, were the best.

Still, it couldn't be "that." Because if it were "that," everything would be undone.

———

"Can you imagine if your life were changed in an instant?" Ian had said as we walked from the parking lot, across the railroad tracks, to my apartment that fall. "A car accident, or anything, can completely change your life."

Ian had seen it happen with two friends, two brain-injured friends, who'd been made different in an instant. He had just recently introduced me to one of them, in fact, at our campus ministry. Still, Ian loved him and the other friend so well, and he cared for them tenderly.

And he didn't know.

———

We neared the hospital, passing my Pittsburgh summer apartment. My heart pounded. After parking and rushing inside, we met the caseworker, a kind and gentle man, just inside the emergency room entrance. He was probably someone's dad. He may have had a son Ian's age. He was doing what was described on caseworker job postings and applications, and he was doing it well. But he was doing it to *us*.

He reminded us that Ian was in surgery, while handing us a few of Ian's things that had been recovered by the paramedics. We held his wallet with the picture of his beautiful little sister Lydia inside. The caseworker thought she was Ian's daughter. Her smile filled his wallet, next to the photo of us huddled on top of the parking garage. He had taken me up there that winter to check out the stars with him. Just across the sidewalk from my apartment, it was one of only a handful of views in our town that let us breathe in the sky.

The caseworker led us upstairs, to the ICU, to the hallway we would come to know well.

And then he told us.

He told us as we stood on the laminate hallway tiles, the hospital drop ceiling perched above our heads.

Ian had been in a car accident, his station wagon crumpled under an SUV. The Jaws of Life had come out, their giant teeth and hydraulics cutting and splitting their way through the white metal. The life-flight helicopter had landed in a field nearby, and the first responders found my best friend mumbling, his body shattered. He was currently in surgery for a massive, traumatic brain injury, and we wouldn't know until the end of the operation if he would live. But either way, some of his brain would be gone.

His parents and his girl crouched in the quiet dark of the waiting room, alongside the other families there whose lives were torn, the wounds still gaping.

I asked Mary for a notebook, if she had one. Anything. A piece of paper. The back of a sales receipt. I *had* to write. She handed me a small, red, spiraled notebook the size of a Post-it note and also a pen. Lydia's little two-year-old doodles were on the first few pages. I flipped past them until I found a blank one, then started writing my letter to Ian on an empty page.

I had been writing letters to him ever since we started dating. I'd filled a journal halfway through already and was planning to give it to him on our wedding day, completely full. The book had been a gift and was covered in soft maroon felt, hand-stitched with tiny yellow and pink flowers and delicate green stems. Inside the cover lay empty sketchbook pages that weren't quite thick enough to absorb ink, making it hard to write in, line-free and delicate. But I loved it. The small red ribbon helped me remember where I'd been and told me where to go next. Writing always kept me close to him.

So writing was the only thing I knew to do in an ICU waiting room. Suddenly for the first time, it became not a secondary way but the *only* way that I knew how to talk to Ian.

After weakly scripting a few words onto the page, my heart started to catch up with reality. I called my dad and wept into the phone, "Dad, please come. Ian is dying." With five hours between their little girl's voice and the other end of the line, my parents left immediately, knowing they wouldn't arrive until well into the night. My sister came. Ian's cousins and aunts and uncles came, hoping to be there by midnight.

A snack machine filled with dry, flaking crackers stared at me as I sat in the corner of the waiting room with Steve and Mary. The wall behind my head separated me from the distraction of the television and kept the other faces in the room a secret. Many of them had just received the same news as we'd received or something similar. Being on the neuro ICU unit meant we were all there for something bad. I didn't want to talk yet, especially to a stranger. We were there just to wait—to wait on something we hadn't even pictured when we woke up that morning.

"Is he awake yet?" I asked Mary as I sat down in the waiting room chair next to her. The exact same waiting room. On another Saturday morning.

Three years and one month later.

Yes, we had been here before. We had sat here before. But this time it was just the two of us. And this time the one in the hospital room was Steve.

Everyone had stayed home to rest after a long night—a long night that told us Steve's brain had been forced to make room for a grapefruit-sized cancerous tumor, and that it couldn't be forced to grow any more.

"No, not yet," she said.

We both put our heads back on the window behind us, the cold glass feeling all too familiar and all too predictable.

While we sat in the still waiting room to hear more about Ian, his three younger brothers were at home, quietly playing video games in the den, waiting by the phone for updates. Lydia had been sent to our pastor's house so that she could play and be happy. She was only two years old.

But word spread quickly, and a friend who lived in the city found us in the waiting room. Staying briefly, she gave us a little Bible, one that we kept with us for months.

David was the next to come. He had just finished playing a concert with his band Willis when he found out. Rushing to the hospital, he may have even driven down the same road, over the same spot, where Ian had been crushed. If he had known to be looking for it, he would've seen the white Kilz paint splashed all over the pavement of both lanes, paint that was supposed to go on the walls of a foreclosed house, not on Route 422 West—a brand of paint I now hate because it nearly killed him, and because its name is too close to what actually happened. For months after the accident, whenever I was in a car with someone traveling that road, I would ask the driver to tell me when we were getting close so I could close my eyes. I didn't want to see the paint that reportedly stayed on the asphalt for months. I *still* don't know where the accident was for sure. I don't want to know. The hauntings in my imagination are more than enough.

David was wearing a blue leisure suit and Converse Chucks when he arrived at the ICU, a common outfit for his concerts.

"You always dress for the occasion," Mary greeted him, laughing at her son's best friend—the best friend whose family had been neighbors of theirs for the first ten years of Ian's life, the best friend who played and fought with Ian every day . . . the best friend who even now has never stopped being one.

What if David had known the night before, when Ian passed up the offer for a ride home, that it might be the last time he ever saw him? And what if Ian, while walking through the familiar streets of Sunset Acres, had known it was the last time he would walk without help? If God had stepped down into the chill of Ian's walk through David's neighborhood that night, and had stopped to tell him His plan, what would Ian have done? Would he have run to my house to hug me and tell me that I had his love always? Would he have made me stay up all night until the time came? Would we have gathered everyone he knew in the same house and tried to laugh . . . but probably cry?

Our families began to arrive soon thereafter. We crowded into the second waiting room, right next to the automatic double doors that led to Ian. We hadn't seen him yet because he was in surgery. They said they would come get us when he could be seen, so we tried to arrange ourselves onto the floor, underneath and on top of chairs with our legs running under the armrests, taking sleep a few minutes at a time.

Then around 2:00 a.m., they came to tell us surgery was over. Steve and Mary went in first, and when they came back, they tried to tell me I should probably wait until the next day to see him.

But I had to go in. And my mom told me, "You need to go in."

I tried to hope, but I feared the worst.

———————

I sat at the dock, waiting for Ian to come down from the vacation house, getting a chance to experience his family's annual, legendary vacation after just eight months of dating. It was my first time to be there, in person, to witness what had become to my imagination a famous two weeks in Virginia. It was actually only the second time I had been with his extended family—the first time for some of them, like the ones from New Orleans that I hadn't met at Easter.

After what felt like waiting too long because I was new to everyone and still felt awkward, Ian finally walked out of the basement through the sliding glass doors, wearing the shortest red shorts ever pieced together by an industrial sewing machine. Head down, laughing hysterically at himself, he strutted down the long, splintery sidewalk made of unfinished wood slats. Every so often he stopped walking and grabbed his belly, throwing his head back, laughing at the mental picture of himself.

I looked at him in fake disgust from the end of the dock, shaking my head in manufactured shame that he would be so bold, so unabashed, so self-confident. His white, un-sunned thighs were given far more attention than they deserved, and his bare white chest gave proof of a summer spent working on a movie set.

But I loved that he loved to be ridiculous. I loved that this guy, who was told by several girls on set that summer that he could be an American Eagle model if only he didn't have a gut, didn't take himself too seriously. This guy, this Tom Cruise doppelganger of a guy, was exactly what I needed.

I didn't know it at the time, but this was the best vacation we would ever have. None of us knew it then, but something happened on that vacation, conversations were held on that vacation, that would stamp it indelibly in the hearts of many of Ian's cousins.

"That year was the best vacation," his cousin Rebekah said years later.

Maybe because everyone was there.

And everyone was okay.

And no one's heart had been broken yet.

Andrea hosted the luau on top of the tiki bar, serving us a huge platter of pineapple and ham. Ian stood behind the tiki bar with his hair pulled into a ponytail, wearing an obnoxious red Hawaiian shirt, serving up Kool-Aid and lemonade.

Jessie and her boyfriend Kai rode in on Uncle Eric's boat, the prince and princess of the luau, her dark summer tan and his Filipino heritage making them perfectly Hawaiian.

We ate and laughed until the sun started to set, and we posed in front of it for photos, capturing a moment of Ian and I that would later rest in a decoupage frame my cousin made. As the sun lowered its head into the body of the lake, its rays spread out across the sky and the luau folded itself into night, ushering us inside to escape the tiny biting bugs coming to life with the darkness.

With that night came an ending to one chapter and the start of another—one that we never would have written for ourselves.

———

I pushed the button that opened the double doors. My mind didn't have a map for this new place that led to where Ian was. Nothing was familiar and I didn't have a compass. My eyes darted around, trying to process and store information. I saw the door to the supply room and the curtains waving in front of me that shielded what was happening behind them.

After we'd passed a few patient beds, they told us we were outside of Ian's. I timidly stepped into the room, brushing aside the thin, blue curtain. I was afraid to see, afraid to acknowledge that his life had been disrupted, afraid to embed a picture in my mind that could be called as evidence proving the accident was real.

I found him in a normal hospital bed, like the ones on the TV crime shows I could never watch because I didn't want to believe those things actually happened to real people. The ventilator hummed as the round accordion pulsed up and down. There were red numbers, screens, and wires leading from Ian's hands to the poles.

Then my eyes found his face.

His face . . .

It looked the same. It was still him. Everything else was covered. Both of his arms were broken, and I could just see and feel his hands past the casts. His head was wrapped in gauze and was oozing, mostly on the right side. His right knee was shattered. His neck was in a brace. His feet were in hospital boots. But his face, the face that was so familiar to me, was perfect. Not a bruise. Not a missing tooth. Not a scratch. It was perfect and it was Ian, and it kept me.

I stood by his side, my mom at his feet. Holding his hand, confused by the bloody patches of gauze on his brain, I stood and cried. This man that I had fallen in love with, who I had hoped to marry within a few months, and who was living a fuller life than seemed possible to me, was broken. He was in a coma, his body completely at the mercy of the doctors and nurses, responsible for moving him when needed, refilling his feeding tube, giving him medicine. Our lives that were independent and easy were dead.

I prayed for him by his bed that night and asked him to come back to me. I kissed his open cheek and pulled myself away from his bed as the nurses came in to help him. I knew I couldn't do this for long and prayed it would not be required of me. Then we slowly left his room, down the hallway centered among the patient areas, many who were in coma sleeps themselves, many who did not even know they were there or that their family was standing over their bed. Much like us. And much like my Ian.

Before that night, I didn't know anything about comas. Every time I would accidentally stumble across a soap opera on television, in between courses or on snow days in high school, there always seemed to be a character in a hospital, either in a coma or lying in bed with an eye patch or something. In those shows and in the movies, the person in the coma was always just sleeping, and then one day they weren't. One day they'd wake up. Maybe they didn't have their memory intact, but they were still awake.

I didn't know if that would be Ian. Or if he would ever wake up.

———

The first morning of October was the first of many that woke us up into a life sadder than my saddest dreams. And while we were all cuddled into each other in the waiting room, our church building on Wayne Avenue was waking itself up, just as Ian's brothers—Ben, Caleb, and Devon—were up and getting themselves ready to make their way to church as well.

During the morning service, our pastor, Mark, led the church in a somber prayer for Ian and described to everyone what his injuries were. Ian's whole childhood had been spent inside those walls—walls he had been painting just a few days earlier to help with building renovations.

Listening to Mark's voice was the first time the boys heard Ian's injuries officially described. Caleb couldn't listen. The reality of the night before pushed him into the men's bathroom and drove his fears out of his heart into big salty drops that fell on his shirt collar.

They left for the hospital after worship to see Ian for the first time, finding him in the same bed where I'd seen him the night before, in the same position, because shifting him onto his side was too dangerous. The ventilator wouldn't be able to work. The IVs would get tangled. The external fixator on his knee would dig into his left thigh. Plus he was simply too fragile.

Not a lot really happened on Sunday. It wasn't until Monday that we received our first conclusive report—a bad one—delivered by a tall, capable looking neurosurgeon. I had never seen him before or looked at his résumé. I hadn't approved his certifications or researched whether or not he believed in natural medicine methods or mainly pharmaceutical. The Friday before, Dr. Okonkwo was absolutely no one to me. But suddenly, he had become my everything. He had seen inside Ian's brain and had spent most of Saturday night there. He knew how bad it was, and he knew the likely outcome of his condition better than I.

In some ways, I suppose, I tried to fit him into the category in my mind that was usually occupied by God, because this man was in front of me, and this man specialized in brains, and this man knew exactly how far gone Ian was, and he could speak to me in words I could hear. He could sit in front of me and tell me exactly what was happening.

We all crowded into the small room—both of our dads and moms, Ian's grandparents, aunts and uncle and cousins. Dr. Okonkwo sat in the chair against the wall to my right . . . and broke my future with ten words.

"Ian is failing four out of five brain activity tests."

My little heart that was trying to keep beating in this new role of mine, in playing hospital host, in praying with the people whose lives would go on being normal in a few days, gave in. My little heart that had held together for twenty-one years caved under the weight of the words that no one wants to hear. Steve knelt before me as I sobbed into his red sweatshirt. I couldn't lose Ian, not like that, not in an ICU bed.

But it was as if his body wanted to die. His brain wasn't responding. And whatever had happened in that white station wagon on Saturday morning, whatever had distracted him enough to cause him to swerve into the oncoming lane of traffic, and then swerve back over to miss it—whatever that was—was killing him.

"Ian needs more than medicine to heal him," he concluded.

Dr. Okonkwo stepped out of the room and took my hopes with him. While others around me were praying for healing, believing that healing could happen, my faith was too small and my mind too weak for such big prayers. My brain was swirling with confusion and sadness, butted up against tiny prayers and glimpses of Lazarus-like healing. All I really knew was this: I, along with Ian's parents and every-body else, needed to prepare for Ian to die. Because if he did die, someone needed to plan a funeral. Someone needed to arrange our lives around a death.

Soon after the bad report, we all went into the room where families go when someone is dying, the room they try to design to feel comfortable, but only to comfort death, not life. The starched, heavy, funeral-home like chairs, the mural of what some artist thought Jesus looked like, the big Bible available for reading and reflection—they all stared back at me, taunting me. Steve and Mary had already met with another social worker, a gentle woman who told us we should start making plans and thinking about the funeral. And since Ian didn't have a living will prepared, we also needed to be thinking about something else . . . whether to keep or remove his life support.

Should we let machines keep him alive?

Or should we let him die naturally?

Kathie, our church secretary and friend, had started calling funeral homes. One of them already knew about Ian. That's how small our town is. Kathie told the man on the phone that we didn't know when, but that Ian was certainly going to die. How did he recommend we proceed under those conditions?

Steve and Mary said they wanted Ian's funeral to be happy, for us to laugh, to watch the movies that Ian had made with David. Their most recent project, "Drowning Melville," would make all of us laugh, they said. That's what we wanted to do. Because that's so much of who Ian was to us. And because sometimes laughing is the best way to be sad.

But in the midst of all this talk about death, his brother Caleb's voice broke in, expressing an opinion that had seemed to be lost on all the grown-ups.

"He's not dead *yet*."

Sixteen years old and with an anger against what felt like a premature death sentence, Caleb believed his twenty-one-year-old brother could still live—which at sixteen is probably good and is normal.

"Nothing bad has ever happened in my life," Ian had said to me just a few weeks before, as we lay on the kitchen floor after a long run. "I haven't even lost a grandparent."

As for me, sitting in that stale room, whose walls had heard countless guilt-dripped and hopeless stories in its past, my faith was only like little gasps of air, little pleas for another breath and another second of strength to keep on. I couldn't help preparing for Ian to die. Every hour meant questions from doctors, questions from guests, and questions from my heart, the biggest interrogator. So I felt like these little gasps of faith needed to coexist with the responsibility to plan for what could be Ian's death and prepare our hearts for what all that meant.

But we still had a decision before us—a decision that felt too big for anyone else but the Lord to make. How in the world, sitting for a few minutes in the family room, could we arrive at the right answer to this God-sized question? We would always be left to wonder the what-ifs: Could he have lived? What would his quality of life have been like? Could he have been happy this way? We couldn't know for sure. We knew that Ian longed for heaven even before his full weight had been set down on an ICU bed, but we didn't want to be the ones to make that decision for him.

So believing in the sovereignty of God, and knowing we could never choose death for Ian, we chose life through support, and gave him the time to do what we hoped would make him better, or would let him die peacefully.

"Don't leave me as the older brother, Ian," Ben told him, saying what he feared might be his last good-bye in the hospital room. He knew he could be seeing his brother alive for the final time.

——————

Dates for us, even years after September 30, 2006, often meant just a ride in the van, with Ian barely able to hear me because of the distance between us inside the vehicle. Being in his wheelchair meant entering through the rear manual ramp and being hooked into the very back of our Dodge minivan. The alterations by the dealer and the way the huge metal ramp dropped the weight of the van made it sound more like a helicopter than a place where people could enjoy road-trip conversations. That meant we would often drive to someplace nearby, just to get out of the house, and after parking I would crawl into the back, sitting next to Ian's wheelchair. It was never comfortable, the spare tire cover digging into my back, my thighs burning. There wasn't enough distance between the floor and the roof to sit comfortably, although sometimes I tried to overcome it by sitting on the armrest of the wheelchair and slumping my spine into a half moon to make myself fit.

But one night, I got him out of the van at a nearby park, and he sat in his tall wheelchair in the grass, pulled as close as possible to a picnic table. I forgot to bring a lawn chair, but even a lawn chair would've been too short to talk comfortably with him, so I sat atop the table. I think that I just started talking to him about his brain injury, because it was the only reality I lived in at the time. I spent every thought inside of a brain injury. And my memories that night went back to the hospital . . . to something that I didn't think I'd ever told him.

"Ian, do you realize we had to make the decision to keep you on life support?"

After a pause, "No."

"We did. But we couldn't take you off of it. We couldn't make that decision for you."

After another long pause, he looked at me with his blue green eyes, the right one a few seconds delayed in focusing, a result of the accident. Although slow, it was still my favorite because of the little orange speck just below the pupil. Then he spoke. Very softly.

"Thank you."

———

As everyone left the family counseling room that day, I stayed, knowing we had just decided to let machines keep Ian alive.

My parents wanted to be with me in that stale room, but I wanted to be alone. Even in the middle of death and the oncoming loneliness it threatened, I didn't want all the people there. I didn't want people back in the room alone with Ian, because if they did something annoying to him, there was nothing he could do to prevent it. He couldn't control who saw him or what they saw. He couldn't pull down his hospital gown when the nurses forgot to adjust it. He couldn't control what he might overhear from staff banter in the hallway.

Soon Ian's family from Philadelphia left for home, thinking they would likely be back on Saturday for his funeral. His brain was still not responding, which meant we were still planning one, even though we all were still praying and believing that something could change.

David took a group of us down to the chapel with his guitar. We opened the doors into the quiet sanctuary, echoing as they closed behind us. We entered reverently, tired and grasping to be hopeful. David's hands strummed the strings and we lifted our eyes and hands and fears upward, asking and pleading for relief.

If God didn't hear those prayers, and if He didn't answer those prayers, we knew we would lose Ian—a thought that was simply too hard to bear. That day my pen turned to puddles in my journal:

> Dear Ian,
> Your dad is right when he says that this is all so surreal. It's so weird to me that I'm here, walking through each day, praying, talking, and mostly sitting, and that you aren't with me. It's so strange that my best friend, the one I share everything with, isn't here next to me. Life is trying to go on, but it definitely isn't as fun without you. I don't even want to think of life at home without you. I just want to hear your voice and hear you say, "I love you, squirt."
> I never saw us here. But here we are. I'm alone on this plastic couch and you're in that awful MRI. I love you. And I hope you read this someday.
> Miss you.

I sat in the sterile hospital hallway later that night, back pressed against the wall with knees tight to my chest. I pushed my cell phone against my ear, hard, because the closer I could keep it to my ear, the more likely I felt that he would come back. It was an old voicemail, just a few days old, and he was singing obnoxiously in falsetto to me on the other end: "I can't see me lovin' nobody but you, for all my li-i-ife. When you're with me, baby, the skies will be blue, for all my li-i-ife." He continued through the whole song, humming and laughing when he couldn't remember the lyrics.

Jen, my friend who was getting married in a few weeks, saw me slumped against the wall, hugging onto the voice that couldn't talk to me. For some reason I had always saved these voicemails, at least the best ones. And now they were keeping me company, even when he couldn't.

I kept listening to them in the cold, empty hospital hallways. And in the car. And lying in bed in the dark, with salt water slanting sideways across my cheek onto the white lace-rimmed pillowcase on my white lace-rimmed twin bed sheets.

Ian. I miss you, Ian.

four

understand that to die is gain, but I don't know what it means that to live is Christ," Mary said, as we sat on Gigi's patio, a warm summer breeze and cloud from the chiminea fire warming our toes. We were a few years into a brain injury and were constantly processing through the loss and change. "If this were just about Ian, we would've told him to give up a long time ago. But this isn't about Ian. It's much bigger than us."

Gigi and Pa had been Mary's college parents in the '70s, when they all attended a Presbyterian church in town. Whoever was running the college parent program at the time matched up a young and witty Mary with the married couple only a few years her senior. The college parents were meant to take a student into their lives and families, inviting them over for dinner, hanging out, and just being someone for them to spend time with. Mary was a college student with a boyfriend in Scotland, she said—which people usually thought was a figment of her imagination. Surely it would be easy to create a make-believe boyfriend living overseas, and still enjoy the implied importance and likability. This overseas boyfriend, though, was in fact very real.

Gigi and Pa quickly became home to Mary, and Gigi a dear friend. I was first introduced to her in Mary's living room, stopping by in between classes to hang out with Ian. She was sitting on the red leather lawyer's chair, laughing. She seemed funny. And fun. I didn't get to hang out with her very much before the accident, but when she arrived at the hospital on Sunday, the day after, with seventeen purses filled with drinks and snacks, I knew she was special.

"That's the face I wanted to see," Mary said.

Over the following weeks I learned why that face, the one that so often made my own face drift into a smile, was so dear. Gigi and Pa had lived in a hospital like ours for months, praying for their grandbaby Livi, who eventually found heaven. They knew what it was like to survive between doctor's reports and to brush their teeth in the hallway public bathroom and to have their understanding of Scripture tested.

Ian still wasn't doing well a few days into this new life. Jimmy and Maelys came up from Virginia from their new teaching jobs to spend time with Ian, in case the doctors were right and he did die. But it wasn't an adventure like the ones we'd shared throughout that unforgettable summer. We just ended up back in the first waiting room, the one with the snack machines and the dry peanut butter crackers that my mom forced me to gag down as often as possible while I sat and waited. I didn't want food because Ian couldn't have food. But I needed it. So my mom, being a mom, always came back from the cafeteria with sandwiches or a soda or a salad. That's what moms do. She was taking care of her little girlie.

Maelys, Jimmy, and Gigi's son Aaron spent time in Ian's room, talking to him and praying with him. Once after coming back from his room, in the hallway, Maelys gave in to the sorrow, tears streaming onto her cheeks and her useless hands. Useless because she, like us, wasn't able to heal him herself.

By Tuesday, we were sure that Ian was going to die. That meant we needed to give his friends a chance to say goodbye—friends he had known his entire life. Like Josh, who was Ian's real-life doppelganger. He even played Ian's doppelganger in the last film project Ian and David made before the accident. In the mockumentary, Josh dressed just like Ian's character, and I creepily felt like I was looking at two of my boyfriends. When my mom came to visit our church, she thought Josh *was* Ian. Even their *own* moms got them mixed up sometimes, looking at them from a distance in a crowd.

Marky and Dave came, brothers who had grown up with the Murphys before moving to Virginia in their late teen years. They and David spent time together in Ian's hospital room, praying for him, praying for God to give them great views of heaven, thanking Him that they knew where Ian would be when he passed. Then Dave, after the focus had been on heaven and Ian's death for too long, asked courageously for God to keep Ian here with them and let him live longer.

My journal, originally meant to be love letters to a man I'd be marrying in a few months, instead became pages for names of hospital visitors, Scriptures that were shared with me, and little blurbs to Ian in hopes that someday he'd be able to read the words scribbled in pencil. The names are fainter now, pages rubbing together after years of being closed against each other in the book binding:

October 2, 2006

Hi, love. Where are you right now? I hope that you can hear us talking to you. Everyone loves you. I want to make a list for you of everyone who's come.

Your family, both grandparents, the Halls, Andrea, Dan, the Altrogges, my parents, Josh, Andrew, Molly, Ned, Dan, Bethany, Hannah, Maureen, Sarah and Kathie, Mark and Dave, Joni, Mr. Logan, Joe . . .

One hundred and fifty three names followed. I don't know if they all came that day. I do know we had the hallway lined. One after another we ushered people in, because we preferred that they part with him there instead of in a funeral home parlor. We saw Ian's friends from when he was a teenager, kids he'd been homeschooled with, friends from our church family in Pittsburgh, Ian's coworkers from his work-study job at IUP, and people he had worked with on his internship that summer.

We all loved him, and we all wanted him to make it.

———————

While Jimmy and Maelys were still visiting, I sat in the waiting room with them, with David, and with Steve. Then suddenly, a doctor we'd never seen before appeared in the doorway, looking for Ian's family. We identified ourselves . . . and were given unexpected news:

"It looks like Ian's made it over the hump," he said.

"What hump?" Steve asked.

We didn't know there was a hump to get over. The day before, we'd only been told again the awful news of how he'd failed so many brain activity tests. And now we were being told there was a hump? And that Ian had made it over?

Yes. Overnight, his brain had started to respond to stimuli. In a matter of a few hours, life and hope and response had breathed into Ian's brain.

"Who are you? The janitor?" David asked in an excited and well-intentioned voice.

We were just so confused—a new doctor, telling us that Ian had made it through the night, a night that now maybe meant life and no funeral. A night we didn't think we would have.

I don't remember what happened next, or what I felt, or what Steve said, learning his son might possibly be okay. I don't think I felt immediate relief, probably because I don't think I ever actually allowed myself to understand how bad it was or processed how truly close he was to death. Ian had to live. Dying just wasn't an option.

We'll never know what he experienced in those few days. Maybe when each of us, after death, is ultimately swallowed up by life, we will watch the scenes from when God reached down inside Ian's station wagon, how God sat with him in the life-flight helicopter, how he and God talked inside his coma. Before the "hump," before he had a chance to live, Ian was somewhere, his mind tucked up inside the cloak of heaven, warmed by the layers of propitiation that took away the fear of death.

And now—where was Ian now?

What were we about to see?

His cousins, aunts, and uncles who had traveled back to Philadelphia, preparing for the funeral on Saturday, were wrong—and in the best way. Ian had been given life, at least for a few days. And while the outcome was still not completely guaranteed, we had all been given a chance to breathe:

October 7, 2006

At times, most times, I have such a mustard seed of faith. But I can delight in knowing that my pathetic seed of faith is tapping into an amazing source of power. I will pray tonight just as I prayed last night, that God would wake you up while we sleep. And I will continue to pray, in faith, that God wants to astound and amaze us.

Death wasn't quite so imminent anymore.

Still, we had decisions to make. Surgeries. Praying for protection from infections. Plus, we'd not even left the hospital yet—Steve, Mary, and I—and we knew we needed to make some sort of living arrangements.

Okay, to be honest, we'd actually been kicked out of the waiting room. In our stupor, we had acted as though it were only for our family—sleeping bags, food, and toothbrushes scattered everywhere. We were kindly reminded, after apparently inciting some complaints, that the room was for *all* families, not just ours.

So a friend generously rented a suite for us to transition into, just a block from the hospital. I don't remember exactly where I slept, but I know the whole Murphy family was there. David had been taking cooking lessons from the Versaces, a local family that made the best Italian meals, like pesto pizza, and he made us a pasta dinner. Mary asked someone to bring pillows for us, and they brought decorative throw pillows made of antique fabric instead of bed pillows. We ate meals that people in the church made for us.

While having a bedroom at the suite was comfortable for my body, my brain and heart had a hard time leaving the hallways of the ICU. I was afraid something would happen if I left. I was afraid I wouldn't do well away from Ian. I was afraid a doctor would come in and say something we should know, or that Ian would open his eyes for a few seconds and no one would be there to see it. I was always cautiously hopeful that Ian would wake up, but afraid it would happen while I was gone. I wanted to be there.

It had been a full week of praying, crying, and only occasionally sleeping. But all I wanted to do was to be there. Just be there.

———————

That following Saturday, my older brother visited with his girlfriend, Ashley, now his wife and mom of three beautiful babies. It was so good for me to have him there. Brandon had always looked out for me, from a distance. He had never been overly concerned about who I dated or who I was friends with. But in very few spoken words, he loved me well. He would only push the teasing so far. He'd take me for four-wheeler rides after spending a long summer day working on the farm. We played basketball together on our cracked driveway, shooting into the hoop my dad had attached just above the garage door. I watched Brandon's high school games, then his college games.

After spending some time in Ian's room, the five of us—Brandon, Ashley, my parents, and I—went out for dinner, after they'd convinced me to step out of the hospital for an hour. At some point before we left, Brandon had asked my mom what I needed, how he could help, how he could change this for his little sister. She told him I probably needed money. So there at the restaurant table, he emptied his wallet into my weak, sad, and unknowing hands. I honestly didn't even remember this moment until my mom reminded me of it years later. Those days were all a fog, lifted only as she spoke. But as I recalled it to mind on her porch one chilly spring morning, I broke. I broke because it felt like God reaching into me, through my brother's love, emptying all that he had, giving it to me. And yet my memory could not even sustain the mere act. Much like the emptying of God into me in so many other ways, grief clouded my memory from holding on.

I never thanked my brother until those many years later—thanked him for giving me his everything, for emptying out to me. I realized what it cost him, and what it could've cost me—a life spent being blind to what was filling those empty hands.

As we neared a week of trying to live past the accident, I tried to be more brave and venture away from Ian's bed, sometimes just down to the lobby of Montefiore, the adjoining hospital. It was separated from ours by only a small walkway, and the lobby was always quiet. I remember walking through the glass tunnel that connected the two buildings and looking at the cars in the parking lots, wondering if their owners were workers or perhaps were also there watching someone die.

Somehow I got the gumption to leave the hospital that Sunday and drive to a shopping center a few miles away. There I realized that life was still happening outside the ICU, 4G Unit. I watched as people rode their bikes on the trail next to the river on an otherwise normal Sunday afternoon. My boyfriend had just spent a week dying, but these people? They were feeling a casual ease and relaxation that had become only a memory for me the previous weekend. They weren't in that hospital just across the river.

But I wanted to get back there. Back to that hospital. Because there, on our floor, everyone was sad. There, everyone's lives had halted.

October 8, 2006
This is real. This situation hasn't gone away and it's real. I think it finally hit me tonight that it's your body on that bed, your chest full of bruises, your little arms that are broken. I just miss you. I've been looking at you all week, rubbing your foot, touching your cheek. But it just hit me tonight that it's your foot and your face that I'm looking at.

I want nothing more than to talk with you and hug you. I miss you and your fleece that you wore so much.

Fighting to trust . . .

The following days, although still slow and heavy and dreadful and difficult, did play host to some events that felt like forward momentum, albeit with an ample portion of caveats.

Around October 8, we learned that Ian's right eye had been responding sluggishly to light, and he was "coughing." It looked more to me like his body was just silently jerking or lurching, but the staff indicated this was a positive sign. He was also responding somewhat to pain. Like when the "janitor" doctor screamed his name and clapped right into his ear, and Ian snorted.

"You can't whisper sweet nothings," the doctor said one day as Jan and I were visiting, after I mistakenly asked if he thought Ian could hear me. He told me I needed to yell into Ian's ear. "Stand right up next to him," he said, "yell, clap your hands, and shout at him." But I knew I couldn't yell into Ian's ear without feeling both completely self-conscious that

the nurses would think me insane, and also because I wanted
to be the sweetness in his life. I didn't want to do *annoying*
things to wake him up. I wanted his memories of our life
together, as well as the future we'd planned—I wanted *that*
to be enough to wake him up. So I only whispered to him
instead. Because girlfriends don't yell.

In the same breath as the yelling thing, however, the
doctor also told me that Ian wouldn't be the same person
when he woke up (*if* he woke up), that he'd surely be left
with significant neurological deficits. It was also the first
time he used the word "coma" to describe Ian's condition.

At that point, I couldn't see the good in having Ian wake
up as a different person.

What if he didn't love me or know me?

What if he lived but had no quality of life?

What if he couldn't understand who God was?

And what if the doctor was right, that I wasn't in Ian's
mind anywhere? They compared his brain to a neatly organized office, where everything was marked and kept in
drawers and totally accounted for. When his car slid under
the SUV, however, a bunch of the filing cabinets shook open,
spewing folders everywhere, and he was left alone in a vat
of gel to try picking up the pieces. He now needed to figure
out which sheet of paper went into which folder and which
cabinet—like the one that made his right thumb move when
asked for a thumbs-up, the universal sign of life in an ICU.
And I, by virtue of being one of his newer memories, would
not be among the first ones to be retrieved.

So the doctor I'd loved when he told us Ian was over
the hump had now become another reason to me for Ian to
get better. I wanted to prove to him that Ian still had me.
I wanted to prove to him that love was bigger than neurons and broken pathways. He thought I was just a random

memory or two in Ian's brain, stuck somewhere in the petro-leum jelly. But when he told me Ian wouldn't remember me, I initiated a new battle and stubbornness in my heart against doctors. They knew more than I did, obviously, but they weren't God. My trust could never be in them.

You show them, Ian.

Show them I'm more to you than that.

But finally, on October 10, eleven days after the acci-dent, I had to go home. My professors had been very gra-cious to me, and even agreed to let me be excused from one class each week the remainder of the semester so I could make the fifty-mile trip to see Ian as often as possible. But as Steve had said, we couldn't live in the hospital. I had school to finish. Steve and Mary had four other children to take care of, the youngest of whom they'd been away from since the thirtieth. I needed to take exams, needed to figure out what to do with my future, and needed to do it without my best friend. I had to be my own puppeteer through this new life.

> October 10, 2006 (blog post)
>
> For all of you that are close to Ian, we feel different empty areas without him with us each day. For me, it's not having my best friend to tell everything to, or his smile that says "I love you." For David, it's the constant laughter and conversations with his lifelong best friend. For the Murphys, it's those loud footsteps down the steps and the voice that makes everyone laugh that isn't there now.
>
> But we must be reminded to thank God, thank God that we are saved, that Ian is saved, and that our joy does not depend on what's going on in our lives. We

are saved. Ian is saved. Our ultimate joy, that deep, insatiable joy, is that we, and IAN, are saved. Be encouraged, all of you prayer soldiers who love Ian so much, be encouraged at how good God has been to us and Ian in the past, and know that this hasn't changed. Think about His promises for the future.

I walked into the Murphys' for the first time since the accident, eleven days and twenty lifetimes later. Steve's parents were there again, just as they had been there the last time I was at the house on the day before the accident. They were playing blocks with Lydia on the thin, blue living room carpet, their white hair welcoming and comforting me. Seeing them, I could imagine how my own parents would be as grandparents.

I hugged them as they greeted me, none of us quite sure of what to say. I wandered into the den, past the video games and computer. The house was quiet, with everyone else either at the hospital or at school. But that wasn't really what made it so quiet. *Everything* was quiet without Ian.

I knew I was supposed to be here. I knew life had to keep pushing ahead, even as I tried to keep pulling it back. What I didn't know was that for the next few months, I would be watching the doors in the house, staring at them, imagining Ian walking through them. I didn't know I would spend Friday mornings at yard sales by myself because I needed the distraction. I didn't know I'd struggle with the crushing weight of my own selfishness, realizing that so much of my sorrow was for myself and not for Ian. I didn't know that even the small things Ian might do to show he was still with me would too soon not feel like enough, because I couldn't have him completely. I didn't know I'd start to worry that

I might have made his healing an idol in my heart, wanting Ian more than I wanted God.

And I didn't know how to "count it all joy," as the Bible says (James 1:2), when everything had been taken away from me. What was that going to feel like? How did a person make that happen?

The fan ticked over my head in the living room as I continued to sit there with Lydia, counting the blocks while she stacked them, wobbly, one on top of the other.

On October 12, Ian had several surgeries. His forearms were broken and needed to be secured with plates. His right knee was also a mess, virtually ripped to pieces. Were it not for the coma, these injuries would've been causing him unbearable pain.

Yet Steve had noticed that Ian's heart rate and blood pressure appeared higher than normal. He wondered if Ian had been given any pain medication and asked the nurse about it when she came in next. She said he could receive them as needed, but so far he hadn't needed any.

He'd suffered a shattered knee, broken arms, and had a drainage tube coming from his brain. And yet he didn't need pain meds.

It was the first time the coma almost felt like a gift.

October 12, 2006 (Steve)
Choked up, I thanked God again for the coma, because his brain registers no pain. If he continues in the coma until the Lord takes him home or until the Lord does a miracle on his knee or till the natural God-designed process (assisted by skillful doctors)

runs its course to a recovery, he'll feel no pain. God is kind.

So, sleep, Ian. We'll wait.

One day back at home after class, my body slumped into the old pullout couch, covered in thick and well-worn upholstery. I had found a few moments when the den was empty, which was rare. This room was Devon's "natural habitat" according to Lydia, because through his years of being a teenager we could always find him there, playing video games or watching *Andy Griffith* reruns.

I rested my head back for those few quiet moments, eyes flickering between a view of the blue built-in book shelves in front of me and the back of my eyelids. The wall to my left was lined in windows with white blinds, open just enough to sneak slivers of sun through the glass and onto my face.

The sleep waiting for me was deep and thick and encompassing as I finally succumbed and walked into unconsciousness. From there my tired body sank deeper into rest, deeper into an afternoon not in the car driving to the city.

Later—however much later—when my body tried to wake up, it couldn't. My eyes tried. My mind flashed on and off like a bulb with a chain pull that wasn't screwed in tight enough. I fought to push myself up, up out of the dense swamp of my sleep, as if pushing a pile of bricks through the belly of a loaded cement truck. It took what felt like forever, my mind telling me to wake up and open my eyes and get off the couch. To fight. To do it.

And when my eyelids finally gave up and opened themselves again, I realized for the first time that Ian wasn't staying asleep on purpose. I knew that what I had just felt and fought through was in some way what Ian felt every time he was asked to do something.

I had wondered so often what was it like in there. Did he feel lonely, lost without his words? I was sure the Holy Spirit was with him, but did he realize it? Did he understand it? What did that look like? Did he wake up a lot in the middle of the night, his eyes only able to look at the ceiling tiles and wonder where he was? Was he scared or confused, and just unable to tell us? Did his mind race and fight to speak but then get rejected on its way to the surface?

I didn't know. I wasn't sure. But I felt in that moment, trying to come back from such a deep sleep, that God had given me an insight into the sensation of a coma, to show me that this sleep of Ian's, this absence of him, was not his choice.

No. He was fighting.

———

Mary and I had just gotten to the hospital, and the nurses were excited to tell us that Ian would be getting up in a chair that day. He hadn't been upright since the accident, so I was excited when I heard—excited until I walked into the room.

There he was, sitting in a chair, but he looked so . . . so disabled. A 5'11", 170-pound man was slumped in a huge, padded, dentist-like chair. On his head, covering his wounds and scars and staples, was a soft helmet, placed there in case his delicate skull was bumped while the nurses transferred him from bed to chair with a Hoyer Lift, an awful metal device that moved disabled people in a fabric sling.

He was sleeping, drool dripping from his open mouth, rendered numb on impact. I remember watching the drool, just staring at it, so angry at that stupid drool and so angry that it was him in front of me. My whole life and future were sitting in that stupid chair, limp under the weight of an underperforming brain, and I could do absolutely nothing to change it.

The strong body that I was so attracted to, with smooth arms and the hint of a gut, increasing with age, was slumped. The man that used to try showing off his acrobatic swing dance moves in his parents' backyard didn't even know what a Saturday night was. His legs were no longer the legs that carried the strut, that strut he had created for himself. Afraid of looking dorky as a teenager, he had trained himself to walk pigeon-toed, not liking the way feet looked when they formed a small V with each step. I used to creepily watch that strut down the hill toward my apartment on campus. I would sit at my computer, looking through the plastic blinds to find him, walking past the dining hall and music building, coming toward me. So noticeable and unblended with the rest, he would walk quickly down the hill in his loafers and knit hat, a smirk on his face, looking as though his legs would surely speed ahead of his torso and send him propelling down the hill.

But now those legs were gone, the right knee completely shattered. His long, brown hair that always looked so perfect and made me smile to see it was matted down into the cuts and forges in his scalp. Clumps that weren't caked with dried blood were shooting like sprouts out of the helmet as his paralyzed lip dripped with saliva.

This was worse than him staying in bed. My gut wrenched at the thought. This meant his coma was not going away. This meant that when they moved his body, he didn't wake up.

I spent hours imagining Ian waking up. My mind created scenarios where we'd stay up all night, talking and catching up on everything that had happened. In these dreams of mine, Ian was not only able to talk, but was able to fully

understand what had just happened and how much I had
given up for him. He was able to remember what it was like
to be inside the coma and could tell me about it. He could
tell me how much his thinking of me kept him alive. He
could tell me I was still important to him. At this point in
his recovery, that's all I wanted to know.

We even started imagining and joking that when Ian
woke up, he would've somehow developed a foreign accent.
Apparently, this is very possible. People have woken up from
comas speaking in a French or British accent. It would've
been the perfect detail for Ian.

As I learned throughout the next days and weeks, it's
good to have hopes, as long as we build the foundation
correctly. This was a delicate balance for my young heart
to make, believing that God could heal Ian but knowing it
wasn't guaranteed. But I needed to learn God's promises,
trust that He would remain faithful, without knowing what
His faithfulness would exactly look like. And I had to learn
these things quickly, because fear was chasing closely behind
me and constantly nipping at my heels.

A reporter who came to see us, after Ian had moved
back home into his mom and dad's house, asked why we still
believed Ian could be healed. The answer seemed obvious to
me. If I stopped believing that God could heal Ian, then I
was forgetting an aspect of God's character clearly revealed
in the Bible. Simple as that. My little heart still swayed, but
it swayed between the reality of what I saw and the hope of
what faith in God can imagine, and tried to find rest in the
middle.

Someone prayed once for the demon inside of Ian to be
removed. If we had more faith, this person said, Ian would
be healed. Hmm. I wanted to find where in the Bible it
told me to pray like that. Where did it tell me there was a

demon inside of my boyfriend? Where did it tell me to pray harder, believe harder, think harder . . . and then Ian would be healed?

How could my tiny body, tiny life of mine, this redeemed, sanctified, purified life, be the one responsible for removing a demon? A God sits above and makes the demons shudder, yet I was somehow responsible for removing it? Could it possibly be my response, my faith, my resolve that would heal Ian? I thought a mustard seed was enough, yet I was being told by those far from our story and far from our home that we needed to believe it into being, that God desired only healing for us.

Some things just didn't add up when stacked against what I was seeing every day.

October 19, 2006

Ian, where are you? I can look at your eyes, but why can't you look back at me? Why can't you sing to me and make me go home when I'm not making any sense because I'm so tired? Where are your big hugs that I loved?

I wish I knew right now how much you love me. I wish I could feel it. I know God loves me infinitely more than we could ever love each other, but Ian, I want to feel *your* love. I want to understand it. I want you to show me how much you love me. I don't want to see you in that chair, with that helmet on. I don't want to think about you looking like that for the rest of your life. I'm not believing that there is any good in this, Ian. Satan is sneaking in on my fears.

Ian, why can't you hold my hand when I put my fingers around yours? Why do you just lie there and not move? If I could just say something to wake you

up and bring you back to us, I would say it. I hope
you know how much I love you. I hope you can feel
right now how much I love you.

Over the weeks I started to see that sadness wasn't
wrong—in fact, sadness was an appropriate response to the
losses we had just faced. For the first few days, I felt pressure to remain in a certain mood or say what felt like the
right things about God. But catchphrases like "God is good"
or "God is sovereign"—all true—are sometimes left empty
when used as a Band-Aid to cover up grief.

Steve sat with me on the couch one night by the fireplace as I tried to write a post for our blog. I was so confused,
because I didn't know in my inexperienced mind how to
match up faith and sadness, sorrow and hope. But he showed
me in his gentle way that it was okay to cry, that emotions
are gifts. Life would be stale and unmoving and robotic
without them. It was okay if I didn't have it all together or
know the right words to answer the questions or respond to
the caring. I could be raw.

And that could be okay.

So I tried to enter into my rawness over the coming
days and weeks. I tried to remind myself that holiness
didn't depend on having clear thoughts, nor did faithfulness
require a superhuman level of energy. In weakness, rather, I
could reach up for the strength that was waiting for me, if
I would allow myself to admit that strength could never be
here without Him. It meant I didn't always have an answer
when someone asked me how I was doing, with that look
in their eyes that meant they wanted more than a "good,
how are you?" I didn't need to act like everything was fine,
because even if my heart and head were a mess, a hibernat-
ing truth existed somewhere down below all those layers of

confusion—a truth that told me He was *for* me because He died for me. Below the messiness of loss was the permanence of the gift and the Giver.

And I needed it to be hidden that deeply, down where it was guaranteed to stay protected and unbreakable. Because without it, *I* would break—especially when the end of October came, the one month mark of Ian's accident . . . time for the first of three weddings that we were supposed to attend between then and December.

The first one was my sister's.

My friend Jen came with me, just two weeks before her own wedding. I knew I couldn't do the trip on my own. I was barely able to do it with the comfort of a dear friend. I knew I would be with my family, but they would be busy. I needed someone dedicated solely to me, to my fragile heart.

Lisa and I had picked out the long, red flowing brides-maid's dress a few months before at the bridal store, and I slowly slipped it on at the church, after getting my nails and hair done. I stood in the bathroom, looking at the wall of mirrors, wondering if the makeup would cover the hollowness hidden behind my eyes. I barely knew how to wear makeup to begin with, and my aunt who sold Mary Kay had come in to help me. I just hoped she didn't notice.

Soon I zipped Lisa up into her white gown that we had chosen together with my mom. It was the perfect dress for her because it fit her petite frame, the small cap sleeves resting on her tiny shoulders. She looked beautiful. She looked happy.

But as we posed for photos, she knew I wasn't really there with her in my head. Everyone who saw me before the ceremony knew. They knew about my loss, then just a four-week-old infant, as well as they could.

I stood one person removed from the pastor during the ceremony and smiled because I loved my sister, but not because I loved standing there.

All I could think about was Ian.

Steve had called me that morning to tell me that he was off the respirator—a huge step. But it wasn't as big a step as if Ian could show up at the church, a three-hour drive from his hospital bed in Pittsburgh. In my imagination it was possible. So as I looked past the guests and to the doorway that remained empty, I imagined him and saw his ghost. He was walking in. His mom was with him. He looked like himself, like he did before that stupid SUV buried him. He had changed out of his hospital-issued gown and showered and removed all of the staples. He'd brought his camera, because he was supposed to be the videographer. He had his gummy smile.

And since my mind could conceive it, it meant that God could purpose it. All things were possible with God, right? Or so I'd been told. Therefore I kept my daring dream alive throughout the whole ceremony. I obsessed with it, waiting for him to show up. I kept waiting and watching the door. If God could heal Lazarus and raise Jesus from the dead, He could surely bring Ian to that church door. Those were the kinds of prayers I'd been hearing for three weeks. Those were the Scriptures that everyone claimed in the cold hospital hallways and chapel. Those were the truths that I was often basing my entire hope around—because without them, I felt left to despair. Without them, I was left only with heaven. And sometimes heaven was too far off to give me hope. It wasn't guaranteed that Ian would walk through those doors. But it could still happen. Maybe.

And yet . . . he forgot to show up for the ceremony.

Jen and I drove the forty-five minutes to the reception in my little silver Focus. I was ushered in past the seated guests by the voice of the deejay, reading words that Lisa had written to each bridesmaid. I don't know exactly what mine said, but it included something about Ian and it made me cry.

I fought to get through the reception. No other wedding would have been possible right then except Lisa's, but with a sister like her, it was worth it. She was the kindest and gentlest sister of all, who could not evoke jealousy in me if she tried and who would do the same thing for me if the situation were reversed. She was the sister who in years to come would invite me to be in the birthing room with her as she gave life to her second little boy, because if I could never have children of my own, she wanted me to experience for myself this incomparable joy.

But even with such a deep love for my sister, my heart was fracturing into tiny little bits—as was Lisa's—with every loving guest who came by to ask how Ian was doing. This was her happy day, and I spent much of it fighting or giving in to tears at the head table.

I did make a concerted effort to dance, forcing my legs and arms into the fast songs, though there was very little of my heart in it. My dad, surely noticing this, finally led me to the dance floor himself. And yet in much the same way as I responded to my heavenly Father, who was leading me into the trial of craniotomies, I started dragging my feet, telling my dad I didn't want to dance, that I couldn't dance. My sad heart couldn't feel the movements of music, because if Ian were there, we would have been dancing together. Instead he was trapped in his bed, trapped inside his brain, trapped inside a life he didn't choose.

When Louis Armstrong wrote "What a Wonderful World," I don't think he knew anyone in the ICU. A simple song that had always made me feel so happy and comfortable was now chafing against my skin. I told my dad I couldn't do it. I couldn't listen to this song. I couldn't get my legs to move into a dance. I couldn't experience something meant to be beautiful while Ian was fighting to live. It had *been* a wonderful world once, but this person I had dived into was gone. And things just didn't feel so wonderful anymore.

Still, my dad was there to hold me on the dance floor. As I cried into the shoulder of his dress shirt, he promised me I would be okay. Yet my heart was exploding. I didn't want to be dancing, didn't want to be learning about shunts and bone flaps, didn't want to be watching death. And I didn't want the photographer to capture my distorted and pained face as we turned.

"Mom, please take that out," I pleaded when I saw the photo years later in the small white wedding album on the coffee table. I couldn't stomach that a memory so stark and so galvanized would be there for others to relive and question and wonder what had been wrong. Even so, through that pain, somehow my dad showed me God that night, taking my little body, leading me into something I felt too weak to do.

And holding me.

———

Ian's progress was slow over the weeks he spent in the ICU. But it was progress just the same. One day in early November, he started to move his arms and toes a little bit. His eyes were still closed in his coma sleep, but he had started to move, just a little.

And best of all, even though the man in the white lab coat had told me that Ian wouldn't know who I was, Ian and God were working up tricks, finding ways to prove him wrong.

Since Ian was attached to a heart monitor, we could see his heart rate displayed on the readout. And we were beginning to notice the numbers going up and down in response to voices and activity in the room. His heart rate record—the highest number to date—was 126. And that was when he was with me. They said, too, that his breathing would get faster when I was there. And later, in the rehab unit, when he would be sitting in the hallway in his wheelchair and I would be standing nearby, the caseworker said that his eyes always followed me wherever I was. He wasn't talking, but he was tracking me. He wouldn't even do that for the therapists.

Still, I missed him so much.

October 23, 2006

When I'm completely living in fear, like earlier today, I'm convinced that you won't remember me when you wake up. The thought is almost too much to bear. Your dad talked to someone who said it's really common for someone out of a coma to regress in memory when they come back. Sometimes temporarily, sometimes not. Ian, what if you don't remember who I am? What if you see me when you wake up but have no recollection of who I am or how much you loved me? I'm scared of our relationship being erased by your accident. Your dad wants to have people talking to you that you've known for years, like your family and David. That doesn't include me . . .

But until you wake up, I'll keep going to the ICU to visit. I'll keep talking to you and telling you I love you. I'll keep praying that you wake up to a full recovery, and I'll keep praying that we can get married someday soon. I'll keep having faith that we'll have a family some day. I'll keep praying that we will spend Christmas together, by this fireplace, drinking hot chocolate and singing cheesy Christmas carols. I want you here next to me, love, and I want to hear you tell me that you love me. Come home soon, Ian.

Doctors said he needed a few more surgeries before they could consider moving him out of the ICU. A vertebrae in his neck had been fractured, for example, requiring a dangerous procedure that ran the risk of paralyzing him. Yet somehow God healed it before surgery. His knee also needed to be fused together—a bloody and difficult operation. But when they took him in, they determined the bone had already fused itself naturally.

Tremendous blessings. True encouragement.

In early November, the doctors put a shunt in his brain to help fluids drain properly. When Steve called to tell me about the surgery, I was in the basement of Davis Hall on campus, getting ready to go into class. I remember him saying that a normal brain gives off a soda can amount of fluids each day, and our bodies just know how to reabsorb it. Ian's brain, however, wasn't letting this fluid go anywhere, so he needed a shunt. They also replaced a bone flap on his skull during the same five-hour operation, since brains tend to notice when they're not protected by a hard case. And we noticed after this particular surgery that he seemed to keep his eyes open more. His family had recorded their voices on a tape recorder, and we played it to him a lot. He was opening his eyes when listening to it, which gave us hope that he knew.

He was receiving much mercy.

He was getting healed over and over again.

And yet often, even as I would thank God for what He was doing, my mind would race back to what Ian was like before the accident, a habit which had a way of stealing any gratefulness. We wouldn't need these new mercies, these canceled surgeries, if Ian had never been in the accident in the first place. We wouldn't need to be trying to rejoice over what God was doing for this *new* Ian if I still had my *old* Ian.

Could I let the old one die? I needed to keep him alive in my memories, but I didn't know how to do it without forsaking the mercy we were receiving. Whenever I pictured the Ian I knew before September 30, I couldn't seem to be thankful for anything.

But what I was doing—much like I still do now—was robbing myself of feeling mercy, of stepping into it as into a quickly moving creek. With the smooth water rushing around my calves, with my feet off balance on the uneven pebbles beneath, I would stumble and catch myself on a boulder in midstream. The current was pushing so hard against me from behind, I couldn't do anything but move forward. But it was mercy that the rock was there to catch me, and mercy that I could look up and see the strong pine trees swaying against the painted blue sky, and mercy that the water was cleansing me and healing me. But instead of seeing those mercies, I would turn around and look at the shore where I had started, and would panic because I wanted to get back there. "There" felt safe. Back "there," Ian was sitting in his khaki shorts and loafers, and he was laughing. If I kept walking forward in the creek, it meant killing the Ian who was back there on that stone, because he wasn't going to make it through the creek unchanged. I tried to see the beauty of the creek, held in by the two rocky cliffs, carved into the feet of the mountains.

But I didn't want to lose Ian.

"I'm living this marriage as if there are two of you," I said as I laid over him, one arm locked next to each of his shoulders, peering down into his tired eyes.

My heart filtered through what he used to look like and what he used to sound like and what he used to say to me. It was as though I was holding these two Ians in separate hands. And as time went on, the old Ian was slipping out of memory. Yet he was right there if I was courageous enough to dive all the way into this life, this fractured, brain-injured life. He was right there if my heart would just be filled with enough mercy to build these two Ians together, so that when I looked at him—my husband—the way I was looking at him right then, lying on the bed beneath me, I really, truly saw him. He was right there if my heart would just . . . change.

"Can you show me the old you, Ian? Can you do something to show me that the old you is in there still?"

"News flash," he said. "There's only one Ian."

Bursting into laughter, I kissed him, this Ian in front of me.

five

Before Ian's accident, he and David had started a filmmaking company named Vinegar Hill, a nod to Jimmy Stewart's birthplace here in our town. David just wanted to jump in and start being creative; Ian knew they needed to make it a business. So they did. Vinegar Hill, LLC.

But then came September 30. And the path that David had laid out for himself, and for Ian, completely shifted.

In that moment, David lost the mind of his best friend, the one that seemed to have been created to be a producer, the mind that could sort through the logistical stuff, a mind that David didn't have. David's mind space was filled with characters and plots and the best way to tell stories. It didn't have room to churn logic. But Ian's did—or it *once* did. And when that mind went into hiding, David was left with a show-stopping decision: pick up and keep pushing forward, abandon the hopes, or take them somewhere else, maybe across the state, where filmmakers were needed, where his company stood a better chance of success. Without his business partner, the prospect of drumming up income in our little town—where even Jimmy Stewart left to make it big—would be nearly impossible.

But David chose Ian.

He chose Ian again and again, day after day, every time he spent his lunch hour next to Ian's bed. He chose him year after year as he watched bigger and better opportunities pass by. He chose to keep loving Ian, even when every gap in business that Ian could've been filling gave him one more reason to question the meaning behind September 30.

But every visit or conversation ended the same way: "Ian, you're my best friend. I love you." Because David kept loving.

Love keeps going.

———

After a few more weeks in the ICU, Ian was ready to be moved to a step-down unit in Pittsburgh. Our hopes were high. Anything felt better than the ICU.

But while the move meant no more restricted visiting hours, no more time spent in the place where death had been so near, it was also terrifying. Unit 4G had become a safe cocoon for Ian. We trusted the doctors and nurses because they were some of the best in the country. We didn't have to worry about Ian not being taken care of well. The patient-to-nurse ratio was one to one. And his nurses had become our friends.

We knew that Tony, for example, lived on Mount Washington, and that he was the first one who shaved Ian's beard because he felt like he should take care of Ian, the way he'd take care of his own brother. We knew that Terri and her husband had helped plant a church in a Pittsburgh neighborhood and were busy reaching out to the community. We knew this place. We knew these people.

Still, leaving meant maybe getting home.

On November 5, 2006, Ian was taken outside for the first time since entering the hospital, being carefully loaded into the ambulance. I was afraid the paramedics would hit a bump too hard on the potholed roads of the old Steel City and the jostling would make him feel unsafe. Any sudden movements might be too much for him. Anything could happen. Couldn't it?

Steve and I arrived ahead of the ambulance and waited in the lobby together, where the walls were covered with artwork done by little preschool hands, dipped in paint and pressed onto pieces of construction paper. Then Ian arrived. We met him as they wheeled him through the automatic front doors.

He looked awful.

His big bed from the ICU was gone, of course, which likely contributed to this horrified first impression. His now-smaller body was perched on a stretcher, held in by big cloth straps that cranked to close, straps that I had only seen before on a truck bed. His eyes were open from the move, so I tried to talk to him in the elevator and hold his hand, to tell him he'd be okay. But my words felt so weak, probably because I hadn't yet convinced myself of them either. He must've known something was changing, something was different, as he laid there with his eyes wide open, wider than usual. He couldn't respond to anything I was saying, but just lay frozen on the gurney.

His new room was smaller too, and somehow didn't feel as clean as the ICU. The walls that weren't familiar and the nurses that weren't Tony and Terri created a new loneliness in me. I instantly didn't trust this place, and my gut didn't like it.

I liked it even less when the respiratory therapist came in, because he didn't seem very interested in Ian and didn't seem that confident and capable, didn't seem to know what he was doing, didn't seem to understand that we had just come from a five-star hospital. I had grown an unexpected allegiance to the ICU, and somehow it had started to feel like home.

This place was not a home.

Immediately this felt like someplace where people go to die.

I didn't want to leave that night, but I didn't have a choice. My shoes put themselves one in front of the other, all the way down the hallway, as I turned what felt like my back on Ian, stepping inside the elevator and dutifully pressing the button. Out in the parking lot, I looked back up at the building to try finding Ian's room, calculating the floors and counting rows of windows until I spotted the one that I told myself was his. The small square of glass looked like all of the rest, but it was different because it was keeping me from him. Under the thick black of the sky, I imagined we were somewhere else—imagined he wasn't falling asleep to lonely hallways and a new unknown.

———

My husband sits at the easel, his left pointer finger caked by the drying, hardening paint as the bottom layers dry. Our neighbor and artist, Carola, gently prompts him in her German accent.

"Do you remember how the sun felt on your face this morning?"

He did.

"I want you to paint that for me," she says, holding the tray of colors he's picked—green and purple and yellow. Music plays quietly. Our thin, white curtains billow slightly as the unusually warm March night air pushes through the window frames.

I sit there watching and drinking tea as he fills the sheet of newsprint from corner to corner with yellows.

"I . . . I really . . ." He works to get the words out. He strains. I listen. I love to listen and wait for his mind. "I really want some orange to . . ." He's drifting. He wants the colors to help him feel and breathe and tell.

He moves on to adding the green of the grass, brushing his left fingers against the paper, creating his memory and giving it life.

Long after he finishes—after his paintings are dried and his hands are clean—his visions will dangle from the walls in our suite, tied to a string I haven't hung yet. To everyone else they will just look like random, unplanned smudges of contrasting colors and lines on a page. But to me they will be lanterns that kill the ghosts of the coma he used to live inside.

One night as I was visiting Ian in the hospital that I didn't trust, the nurse came in and sat by his bed to give him medicine through the port in his stomach. They had replaced his IV with a feeding tube, creating a scar that now gives him two belly buttons. But the nurse spilled medicine all over his hospital gown. A lot of it. And did nothing. She just walked away as he laid there, soaked in his medicine.

Soon we started noticing even more things being done incorrectly to Ian, or not being done at all. As if seeing him in this weakened condition weren't enough, having him treated by less than capable and caring hands was just too much. So when we received word after two weeks that he could move to a rehab institute for children twenty-one and under, we felt like we had been handed the gift of life.

He would have therapy every day.

He could wear his own clothes.

He'd be able to take a shower.

If he got well enough, he would even be able to swim.

So we made another move, this time excitedly. Mary and I packed Ian's suitcase, eagerly putting his own clothes inside it—no more hospital gowns! And as soon as we arrived, the place felt good. Safe. It even smelled wonderful.

But little more than an hour later, his new doctor came into the room and reversed our newfound excitement. She told us, after evaluating Ian, she wasn't confident that she could take care of his medical needs there. She revealed to us some things that were happening inside of him, things we weren't aware of, deficiencies he was suffering. She gave us some information which led us to conclude that his care at the step-down unit had been so poor, they were actually killing him.

Ian was dying.

And that meant loading him back up into the ambulance, back into a hospital gown, back to the original hospital.

He wouldn't be sent back to Children's for several weeks, not until after Thanksgiving. But his return to this facility—the clean-smelling place where we'd first felt like

Ian was making a new start in his recovery—set us on a new, uphill path of hope. The tall, skinny guy who ran the Zamboni-like machine down the hallways several times a day would saunter by, smiling, and say, "He's looking good today!" above the hum of his floor sweeper—the man who made it smell not like a hospital. He was right. Ian was looking better. Every day.

On November 29, nine weeks after his accident, he showered and wore his own clothes for the first time.

The next day, November 30—the one-year anniversary of our first date—he began what would become an ongoing regimen, three hours of therapy each day, with a new doctor and a confident staff who seemed to think of their work as more than just a job. They really seemed to want him to get stronger.

He even got to sit in a wheelchair, one that we could push around. Mary had so wanted him to be able to go outside, to feel air that wasn't vacuumed through a hospital HVAC system, and the wheelchair gave her the first chance to do it. She bundled him up in his gray knit hat with the thin yellow stripes, and rolled him through the double automatic doors that kept patients in and normal life out. Twenty-one years before, she had carried him through doors like these as an infant, loading him into their '70s-era Volkswagen. And now, she stood by her firstborn's wheelchair under a winter sky, blanketing him against the cold, watching his eyes stare up at the moon behind the bare tree branch that canopied the sidewalk, hoping that something in the cool air was strong enough to breathe life into a coma.

I remember how nice it felt to see that green fleece blanket resting over his sheet when I'd walk into Ian's room. Light green and smooth on the side opposite the fleece, it was the first time he could use something from home. This

place had a washer and dryer on-site, to help get the medical smells out in a good soaking of Tide. I loved washing his
clothes. Laundry felt normal, even though it was done under
the guise of a washroom in a rehab institute. I washed the
soft, comfortable clothes he wore to therapy and in bed.
Those were all he needed. He didn't need and couldn't wear
jeans—first, because he had nowhere to go in them, and second, because their tightness would be too hard to work onto
his legs. So I washed the blanket along with the shorts that
often had nasties on them: urine, poop, medicine, vomit,
food. And hoped their old Murphy smell would remind Ian
of a time and place he still wanted to get back to.

On December 2, I wrote a post on our blog and titled
it "He's in There." We didn't have many signs that he was,
actually, but on this day I was encouraged because he was
tracking photos with his eyes and moving his hand up to
grab his gown. His right eye had never really closed since the
accident. The bulk of his brain injury was on that side of his
head, and whenever he moved, even small movements, they
usually happened on his left side. But our only true window
inside was through his open right eye. And when it began to
move a little, we began to dream.

But while Ian was lying in bed with an eye that wouldn't
close and a brain that wouldn't open, I was doing my best
to finish college. I had made it to the final few weeks of my
very last semester, and the graduation ceremony was getting closer. But to think about going to a party the night
before, then walking across the stage and celebrating over
lunch with my parents afterward, felt both unfair and selfish. Celebrating *anything* was the last thing I wanted to do.
Receiving my diploma when Ian should have been there
with me made no sense at all.

Then on December 6, we received news from our university that they would grant Ian his diploma because of the extensive work he'd done on his internship just before the accident. His name would be announced at the ceremony, where his best friend David was scheduled to give a speech. Seats would be reserved for Ian's family, and David would receive the diploma on his best friend's behalf.

But the only thing that really mattered that December was getting Ian well . . . and trying to imagine how to celebrate a Christmas that was missing so much in the way of joy.

Lydia, Ian's little sister, was just shy of three that December, and was starting to ask to go visit her brother. "Will he squeeze my hand?" she asked. We hoped so, sitting there beside him on Christmas morning in the hospital. We were all there: Ian's parents, four brothers, little sister . . . and me. Lydia especially was very caring with him, touching his arm and asking questions—"Do you think he's comfortable?"—questions that showed even her little two-year-old heart cared deeply for her big brother.

All of us being together was special, as it should've been. Still, I couldn't help but remember what Christmas had held for us the year before. I couldn't help but remember how, right after the accident, I had told God that I couldn't make it until Christmas.

One of our first dates the year before was to see Christmas lights at a park. He had wanted to kiss me that night, but held in. We had also been together at an ugly sweater Christmas party I'd hosted, complete with my roommate's incredible spinach artichoke dip and lots of laughter. Everything I loved about Christmas was becoming everything I loved about falling in love. And all through-out that amazing month and season, I made my poor new boyfriend listen over and over again to Mariah Carey sing-ing that song because, like she said, all I really wanted for Christmas . . . was "you" . . . was Ian.

We made a Christmas chain together, the kind people make when money is tight. We wound the red and green construction paper strips together, each of them carelessly cut at different widths. We wrote messages to each other on the inside, but kept them a secret until they were ripped off, one for each day. Some messages were jokes; some were rules like "No CNN until New Year's," and some were ran-dom stick figure drawings.

Ian also drew us a fireplace on computer paper and hung it on the wall behind our TV. Next to it we placed our stock-ings, each with a name written in puff paint. Ian, of course, bought one four times as big as a normal stocking, because when he passed it in the Dollar Store, it made him laugh too hard to keep walking past.

Finals came, and when they went, it meant going home to my parents' house. Ian spent time in Philadelphia with his extended family, and I felt special because he gave me his dad's cell phone number so I could call him. But we couldn't stand being apart for too long, and so I came back to my apartment early, before classes started, just so I could see him.

That first New Year's we spent together wasn't at a big party or crammed into a city street. He wanted to take me out to a quiet dinner at a little Italian restaurant in town. Wearing his light pink, button-up dress shirt from a thrift store, he picked me up, and I made my special sunroof entry into his car. I remember as we ate we talked about mostly mindless things, and then we talked about God. It was sweet and exciting, new and yet increasingly familiar.

After our dinner of Alfredo and a plate of lasagna, we headed back to my apartment for my first-ever screening of a Murphy family classic, *It's a Wonderful Life*. We sat on my poorly made apartment couch, its light tan background and weird geometric patterns holding our weight.

That New Year was comfortable. We were only a month into dating, but it seemed so perfect. It seemed like it would last forever. January 2006 came into us sweetly and with promise.

Christmas 2006, though, was forced to be different. Ian wouldn't be getting me the new Bible he'd promised. He wouldn't be writing secret notes to me on the Christmas chain.

And he wouldn't be coming home with me on Christmas, like we had hoped.

On Christmas Day, after we opened gifts with Ian at the hospital, Ben and I drove back to the ICU and delivered homemade cookies to the families on 4G. Our old waiting room was empty, but belongings were scattered everywhere, which meant someone would soon be coming back sad from a hospital room, but would find a special gift, just for them . . . from someone who knew their sadness too well.

And on New Year's Eve, while other people our age were probably at parties, I sat in a chair next to Ian's bed while he slept. I had gotten special permission to stay overnight on the window seat in his room, opposite of his bed. I couldn't think of him being alone in that rehab institute on that holiday night, and I didn't want to think of myself being without him either, sixty miles away at a party.

So I tried to get a few hours of sleep through the evening, tucked up in a chair underneath the hospital TV.

Because of the double doors between his room and the hourly check from the nurses, my slight sleep was often interrupted by the opening and slamming of sickness. But when the ball dropped, I remember looking to my left where Ian was comfortably asleep, wishing he would just open his eyes. Wishing 2006 had never ended like this.

Wishing 2007 would change it.

———

When we were dating, I remember our friend Sarah telling me that she was shocked to see Ian showing affection to someone. She was used to him being the sarcastic life of the party. Willing to talk to anyone, but also not shy about saying funny things that may or may not be taken well. But he was in love when he was with me, and this friend she had known and been homeschooled with since she was little was actually outwardly showing his love.

That's the Ian I fell in love with, the one who showed so much affection to me. He would gently hold my hand—as gently as he could, considering he has the fattest fingers in the world. It often felt like a vise grip, but it was still so sweet.

Then for a few years, that hand didn't have life. It couldn't squeeze when it wanted or reach out to find mine.

That's different now.

The same Ian who seven years ago shocked Sarah so much by the changes she saw in him is still marked by gentle affection.

It's easy to forget or overlook things like that, because some of the greatest benefits of marriage are actually the smallest. I had missed Ian's affection for so long after his accident, but was surprised, even after it came back, how quickly I moved on and began to overlook it.

One night as I lay falling asleep, chin tucked gently into his shoulder crevice, I felt his warmth that entered in between each finger as his hand clasped mine. Our ten fingers stayed linked as sleep drifted onto our eyelids, forcing them closed.

Falling asleep holding a husband's hand. A gentle husband who is so happy to fall asleep with hands bound. I don't ever want to grow blindly accustomed to that.

I'm thankful to be married to a tender heart.

———————

For the next four months—January through April—we lived at Children's, and Ian's schedule continued to be filled with therapies. He was working at sitting up on the exercise mat and learning to wipe his mouth with a washcloth they always kept nearby. He was also working with a speech therapist, Val (his first of many speech therapists). Val pushed Ian, not willing to give in to his stubbornness. I sat through many of their sessions where Ian wouldn't, or couldn't, open his eyes. Val would put her petite hand into a fist and rub it hard on his chest cavity, trying hard to stimulate him enough to make it worth a therapy session.

On January 17—finally, for the first time—he uttered noises that sounded like words, an "uh huh" escaping through a cough when a nurse asked if he was comfortable.

His hair was also starting to grow back in, after being shaved for surgeries and procedures, all except for one little bald spot—a spot I jokingly told him would look great if it remained bald. Fortunately for Ian, he started with a full head of thick, shiny hair, and once his diet returned to normal at Children's, his nails and hair started growing like crazy.

But at the end of January, I confessed to my journal that watching Ian in his hospital bed that night felt like the first time he wasn't really there with me. I saw the Ian that was lying in the bed, but that's all I could see. I couldn't see the healthy Ian. This was a new loss of memory for me, a new kind of sensation. I feared I had lost a measure of hope. And I knew that was something I couldn't give up. I even passed on a job offer from an ad agency in Pittsburgh that I received a few days later. Because if he went home, and my work held me in the city, it would be too far. I wasn't ready to be away from Ian.

My community had shrunk to whoever lived at the Murphys at the time and my boyfriend lying in a hospital bed. I wanted to be happy for people whose lives were moving on, but any attempt to rejoice or invest my attention in them fell flat, sucked out by my grief. Finding it hard to distinguish between grief and self-pity, the easiest option was to keep my thoughts in my mind and script them out in my journals, because I had no idea what I was experiencing and had no category for it. I tried to dig myself into the Bible on my good days, and bury myself in Spurgeon on the bad ones. Because on the bad days, I simply couldn't understand a God who was okay with shunts and feeding tubes, so I read the words of those who had Him more figured out than I did.

Friendships were hard to work on because I wasn't home that much. And when I was, I was thinking about how I wanted to be with Ian. So I did my best, but I know that I neglected and pushed away. I couldn't help it. I didn't want to be the needy, distracted friend that no one quite knew how to care for. I thought the man in the wheelchair in Pittsburgh was the one who needed me the most, and I just didn't have it in me to put forth the work and initiation that friendships require. Fortunately, my friends knew better than to take my absence personally, and they did their best to keep pushing in.

My family, I think, struggled the most to understand what kind of care I needed and why I wasn't really there when I was home, why I always seemed distracted. They saw a different sister and daughter in me after the accident. And not having lived in an ICU themselves, they didn't know what words to use in offering comfort to me.

Part of me was empty, and I couldn't hide that emptiness. I couldn't hide the fact that when I was home, I would rather be with Ian—that all I could think about when I was away from him was what I was missing. I would play out in my mind how horrible it would be, if he were to wake up, and I was still two hundred miles away when it happened.

Lying in the bedroom where I'd slept as a little girl, looking up at the ceiling I'd once covered from corner to corner with magazine ads, I imagined all that might be happening in Ian's room without me there. Guilt dripped into my bed sheets as I thought about Ian lying by himself in a hospital. He couldn't tell me yet that it was okay for me to leave, that he *wanted* me to leave so that I could be refreshed. Unlike now, when I ask him if I can stay at my parents for an extra night to spend more time with them, and he says through the phone, "There's nothing I'd rather you do," he didn't have those words then. And so in the absence of his words was guilt, and my guilt showed up in my parents' living room as a silent, distracted daughter. I could feel it at the time, but I didn't know it was so obvious, not until my brother told me on the phone once, "I want the old Larissa back."

"I do too," I said, even though I knew too much had happened, and too much was still going on.

I started to be afraid that my family was taking it personally, when for me, I was just trying to keep my life together.

I was just trying to sort through the fog that had settled over my thought processes, trying to exert enough mental energy to remind myself that God could still heal Ian. I wasn't self-aware enough yet to understand how my suffering was affecting my family. And quite honestly, had I known, I may not have even been able to change. I was walking through a dense haze, trying to respond like the Bible says I should, but I really had no idea what I was doing.

There was only so much my mind could handle.

"I know the Bible says somewhere that God won't give us more than we can handle, right?" I asked our pastor Joe during our first post-wedding counseling meeting.

Laughing, he said, "That's not really in the Bible anywhere. But it does tell us that God will provide grace for all that we're called to do."

Oftentimes my family could see that I would rather be with the Murphys, like that first Christmas after the accident. I only stayed at my parents' for a day, and in the cloud of grief I lived in, I couldn't see what that said to my family. I couldn't see what they felt when I left quickly the next morning. To them, I think, it looked like I was choosing the Murphys over them, over this family that loved me so hard, upsetting a Christmas Eve and Christmas Day that had been the same way for twenty-one years—with M&M's appearing on the tree in the morning, listening for the bells at night, and waiting to hear the song on the record player before we could leave our rooms and come open our presents.

We tiptoed around the obvious—that my boyfriend was never going to be the same—and instead talked about antique Oliver tractors my dad wanted to buy and restore for his collection. Unlike now and unlike then for my siblings, coming to my parents' house wasn't a vacation but instead required guts—guts to believe that God was with me even in the mountains while Ian was so far away.

What I didn't tell them, what I should have told them, was that somehow the Murphys kept Ian alive to me, that twenty-one years of Ian memories lived in their house and in their presence. Ian's name was in their conversations and in their grief. In a way that my family simply couldn't, being with Steve and Mary meant remembering this son of theirs who used to yell-sing all through the house, who loved playing golf, and who was the most like his mom. ("We used to joke that Ian got all of both of our bad habits," Steve told me one day, joking.) Being with the Murphys meant being in a shared grief. The idea of not knowing what to say was no stranger to them. They understood what made so many things impossible now. When Mary opened up her split-entry home to me, with its antique plates hung on the walls, she opened up a home for my grief, an alternative to having it rumble around inside walls with people who had no way to really understand. Inside the darkness of her first little baby's coma, she opened up life for this young woman she was just getting to know.

Before the accident, she had opened up her home for me to stay over the weekends when I came home from my internship, while Ian was three hundred miles away in Lancaster. For each visit she would lay soaps and little gifts on my pillow, making me feel welcome in a home that would in a number of months become a permanent place for me to feel welcome.

And now, they were some of the few people who understood and fully supported my decision to stay with Ian, now that he was someone so different. This obviously made a few people uncomfortable, like when someone told me I needed to keep moving on with my life, that I couldn't just wait around for Ian. Or the time when someone told me I was wasting my life where I was, sitting at my boyfriend's side, when I had so much more potential than that.

All they did was make me dig my feet into the cold tile floors of that hospital even further.

Whatever this "potential" was or whatever I was missing in my life while waiting around with Ian—it all fell on deaf ears. I *couldn't* leave him, didn't *want* to leave him, because he was my best friend.

And best friends don't just leave.

I could actually blame my parents for my decision to stay, because they had taught me well from childhood that love doesn't give up. In the days when my hair fell to my waist and my sister lived in her ballet show tutu, we would dance around the brown-paneled living room as our mom's record player spun The Bill Gaither Trio children's album: "Love never gives up, love never lets down / Love keeps on trying through smiles or frowns / Love never says die, even when it gets rough / True love just never gives up!"

As our mom watched her two girlies, prancing on the brown carpet that I used to secretly cut with scissors to the slow, intentional rhythm of the bass line, she would never have guessed her lessons were preparing me to stay next to a man in a coma. But just as our mom loved our daddy through unasked-for troubles and tragedies, she was unknowingly teaching us that love doesn't walk away. She was showing us that just because hospital visits and doctor's appointments come along, leaving is still never an option.

My siblings and I grew up in a home that valued marriage and ate dinner together every night. We grew up under a dad's words that told us we could never let anything come between us, even when we left home, married, and moved away. The one thing that would kill him, he said, would be abandonment and strife. My parents modeled the kind of heart that commits and works through the unexpected, the kind that prepares for *being* prepared. And I would need that kind of shaping, that kind of molding and encouragement, when I didn't have words left anymore to fight through my grief.

And I would need this family to hold on to me when I simply couldn't pursue them myself.

"Use the knobs, that's what they're there for," my dad's voice broke into the 1990 home video from behind the camera. It was my fifth birthday. He had made me a miniature hutch for our play kitchen in the basement, and my sister and I were struggling to open the long, skinny drawer that was sized to the width of the hutch countertop. Distracted from my new white Barbie Ferrari, meant to deter my jealousy of Lisa's red one, we paused from awkwardly yanking on the drawer to respond to our dad's voice.

Just before he offered his instruction, my dad the videographer had cut over to a view of my mom. She was standing in front of the big bow window in our house that looked out over our small front yard, three big trees separating it from the country road. Just beyond the road was a short meadow, flanked by a small patch of trees I used as my fort. It was the part of the yard where we played Devil in the Well because the two maple trees had the perfect limbs for climbing, and because for some reason we never realized just how creepy the title of our game was. It was the yard where our little feet shuffled to keep up with my brother's soccer dribbling skills, later going inside with grass-stained soles and knees.

If it had been up to my dad, two of those feet that sprang through the yard might not have been there to get dirty. After my brother and sister were born, he thought our family was complete. One of each, he had said, was a perfect family.

"No, someone is missing."

My mom's maternal nudging was right. And nine months and a few weeks later, I arrived exactly on my dad's thirtieth birthday. All seven pounds and six ounces of me shook up a house that for three years had become settled and cozied into its own normalcy.

As my dad had turned the video camera to my mom during my birthday party, it was clear that being one year removed from the '80s hadn't allowed enough time for her perm to settle. Her profile reflected the trend. She was standing with her arms crossed, watching her girlies struggle with the knobs. Her knit, darkly colored vest lay over a black turtleneck.

"Hi legs," said the voice from behind the viewfinder.

In return a shy smile, "Hi."

All of my home videos captured these sweet moments, and so did my memory. Walking into the kitchen from my bedroom down the hallway, I often found my parents under the kitchen light, hugging after a long day, after the meal had been cooked and the three kids had been fed. They would kiss and I would run away screaming, because parents weren't really supposed to do that. It felt horrific to see any affection between them, because that meant they liked to do those "things." Horrific as it was, though, it stayed with me—my strong, healthy dad wrapping my tired mom into his arms, hugging her, comforting her, enjoying his wife. He was intent on taking care of her, and she was delighting in being taken care of.

In many ways, that's simply all I ever wanted.

———————

Back in the hospital, conversations started to turn toward Ian moving home. The doctors said he was suffering from a common condition of many long-term hospital patients, something at least casually referred to as "ICU psychosis." It can be caused by several factors, mainly environmental things like being in a stale hospital room, having fluorescent lights constantly shining on you, suffering sleep deprivation from nurses always needing to check on and monitor you. Until it's encountered personally, it sounds crazy. But Ian was shutting down. He wasn't doing anything at therapy.

And therapy, at that time, was his main reason for still being in the hospital. So if he wasn't really participating— which he wasn't—the determination was made that he'd likely be better off at home. He was medically stable enough for it, and we could hire a nurse to help with his care.

He needed home.

Which meant relief.

It meant no more trips to see him every day. No more sacrificing time with their other children for Steve and Mary. No hospital monitors or staff or restricted visiting hours.

It meant hope. Because even though he was shutting down mentally, he was healthy enough to come back to Warren Road. God was not done.

So I started packing up his room at home to get ready for his highly anticipated arrival, just in case this glimmer of hope might actually come true. But I didn't want to upset the arrangement of things in his room too much, even though much of it needed to be put into bins and packed away. He'd obviously placed things exactly where he wanted them to go. He'd put the incense burner on the glass book-shelf and filled the filing cabinets with his schoolwork. He'd started his growing collection of guitar picks and stashed them in an Icebreakers gum holder. He'd decided where on the wall to hang the black and white vintage photo of his grandpa playing football, as well as the vintage thrift store boxing gloves.

It was all so Ian.

And so even while we made room for him in his parents' home, I started to give room in my gut to what I'd been bat-tling and trying to avoid. I needed to allow another mixture into my heart. I was scared that this Ian was gone, scared that I would never hear his voice again, scared that he wasn't really in that body anymore.

Yet all I wanted was for him to come home.

Usually those moments were at his bedside or falling asleep at night in Lydia's room. Much like now, there were good brain injury days and bad brain injury days. In early March, for example, there were a few days when Ian didn't really seem like he was with me. He was awake when I was visiting, but he wasn't really awake. I remember looking into his eyes, trying to search through them for proof that the old Ian was still in there, trying to peel back the layers of surgeries, scars, and blood that were burying the original Ian inside. His eyes were the one part of him that should still let me in. I used to get so dumb when I'd look into his eyes, back when they were both in sync, when he could make each of them shift to look in the direction his brain requested. After the accident I tried and tried for that to happen. Earlier, when his right eye was open all the time, red and unable to dilate, I'd fill it with goop each night in hopes the cornea wouldn't be damaged. I so wanted to climb back into those eyes that hopefully led back into his heart.

But somehow, living right next door to the fear that Ian wouldn't remember me, was also the very real excitement that God hadn't finished with Ian, that He was still listening to us. Even in my most desperate times, He kept me from sinking into total despair. So with each exhalation of fear, I breathed in more of God as He moved and created in us and held me into love.

The love that keeps going.

———————

His birthday gift from his mom was a coupon to redeem for a picnic, meal of our choice, date and time of our choice. And so being date night, we stop at Mary's house for our basket filled with chicken salad sandwiches, brownies, milk, and lemon water—at Ian's request.

The sky is teasing us with passing dark clouds, so we opt for the park with a nearby pavilion. We take just one thing out of the basket at a time, in case we need to pack up quickly. After an hour of watching the clouds, and eating and talking, we decide to risk it and settle on a blanket under a strong and sprawling tree.

I want to capture the moment, so I brush past Ian lying on the blanket, looking back at the tree as I walk backward, camera in hand.

"You look beautiful in that skirt," he said.

After a quiet thank-you, I snap the picture, a smile behind the hands holding the phone. I walk back over to the blanket, lying down next to him, smiling yet.

"I can't believe I'm so blessed to have such a beautiful wife." Noticing I'm cold, he pulls the blanket up over my shoulder, simply loving me.

Turning onto my back, looking up at the huge tree, I can't seem to wipe the smile from my face. God had known exactly what my heart needed that night. He softened my heart as He softened Ian's, and gave us a sweet and beautiful moment of feeling so deeply the joy of being loved, by each other and by our Father.

In a nagging week that had "brain injury" running through my thoughts too many times, tired from work and spending time with our little nephew Paladin, here was a moment of peace. Here was a moment of rest.

And so we rested. Rested in His love.

––––––––––

Moving Ian home meant building an addition to the Murphys' house. So within a short period of time, the yard became flooded with excavators and construction workers and plumbers and electricians—people from our church who were gifted in such handy, professional trade skills. The construction *outside* meant Lydia and I spent a lot of time together *inside*, watching the workers through the French doors of the den or playing with her Fisher-Price house while she sat with the elastic bands of her butterfly wings wrapped around her shoulders.

Frank, who eventually became Ian's first caregiver at home, coordinated meals for all the workers, and a local pizza shop donated pies on more days than I can remember. The floors were coated in men's work boot tracks, and drywall dust flitted in the air against the pressure of ceiling fans.

God was using His church to be His hands and feet.

But as much of a gift as Ian's homecoming would be, I wanted all these intermediate activities to end—all the business-like decisions, the practical preparations, the changing around of rooms and disruption. I just wanted Ian to come silently back into my life and into my days. I knew the work meant progress and no more hospitals. I was enthusiastically happy about that. But it also meant that Ian had needed to go there in the first place, and that he was coming home on a stretcher in an ambulance. He wouldn't be driving home. He wouldn't be walking in the front door, jumping loudly from the top stoop to the floor, bypassing the three steps in between.

I wanted to wake up and realize that this was all a long, encompassing dream. I wanted to wake up and realize it wasn't me who'd been sleeping in the loft bed above Lydia's Pack 'n Play. I wanted to wake up and be told that the accident had never happened, that he'd never slipped out of my life, that we were back together like always, this close to beginning the life I'd always wanted.

Brain injuries have a way of making hearts flip-flop between hope and the reality of loss.

On one trip home from the hospital, I stopped at a department store, trying to distract myself with a shop full of clothing and other things I didn't need. Like most any girl, I had loved slowly turning page by page through magazines full of white and ivory wedding gowns, and I already knew what I wanted to wear at the end of the aisle, long before I met Ian. Interestingly enough, I happened to find that kind of dress in that store for only $20, a few miles from the hospital and oceans away from any chance of a wedding. Still, I grabbed my size and cautiously walked to the dressing room—cautiously because I knew my heart was on the line.

I knew if I put it on and looked in the mirror, my emptiness would only deepen.

But it did fit. Perfectly. And so I snuck it into my cart. Pretty soon, I was standing in line, queuing up toward the cashier, preparing to go ahead and buy it. But even as I waited behind the two or three customers in front of me, my mind drove me back to the hospital and found Ian still lying there, still so very sick. I had a wedding dress in my cart that felt like it had a better chance of being worn in twenty years by Lydia than in one year by me. And the illogic of the situation raced through my heart like ice water. Reality and a brain injury forced my hand onto the dress I'd folded across the cart, and I filtered back into the store to return it to the rack.

———————

That March, I had my first birthday without Ian. My mom came to spend the day, and even stayed with me for the night in the Heasley House—a place where patients' families could stay instead of going to hotel rooms. Again my journal was etched with words longing for Ian to surprise me, for God to surprise me, by bringing Ian alive again on that day, because it was a day I didn't want to spend without him.

March 14, 2007

Hi, love. There are flowers resting in front of the mirror on my dresser, but they aren't from you. I found a birthday card from you, but it's from last year. I hope your message would be the same.

I can't help but cry tonight. I don't understand why you're still gone or why I'm still sleeping at your house instead of you. I'm sick of other people taking care of you and getting you in and out of bed. I'm tired of daydreaming about the day that you wake up. I'm tired of the reminders that this is in fact real and that it's happening.

I went to dinner with your family tonight, but you weren't there. We celebrated my birthday, but you weren't there. And all I can think about is how terribly sad this is. All that I have now are your letters, your words. I can't grieve that you are gone because I want to believe that you are still here. But I can grieve that you are missing my life and I am missing yours.

I would rather God take you home than leave you like this.

Whenever I visited him, I would push him in circles around the halls of the hospital in his new chair that weighed almost the same as my body weight. Sometimes his eyes were open on the walks and sometimes they were closed. We circled the same hospital rooms, the same rooms with sick kids and families who'd rather not be there. The same nurses were in the station. The same kids were in the lounge with the fish tank the length of a whole wall and the computers that slowly connected to the Internet. But with each lap we took, I felt an opposite reaction of loss, because each lap in his wheelchair ticked away another three minutes that were different from the three minutes our friends had just experienced in their college classes or at home with their new spouses.

All the same, I did want to pass my time with him; I didn't want to be absent and waiting for him. But I just wanted a sign so that I could prepare my heart for what was next. I had been just sitting there looking at him for six months, watching him sleep, hoping for him to awaken, all the while having no idea if he even realized I was there with him, or would *ever* realize it.

"When Ian gets better, he'll come on a picnic with us too," little Lydia told me one day while the two of us were out. But his brain was still floating around somewhere between the world we were living in and the world where people go when they're in a coma. I didn't know anything about that world, whether it was scary or peaceful. I didn't know if it was comfortable or lonely, gray or filled with colors that maybe I'd never even seen. I longed to know that he was okay, and to know that wherever he was, God was with him, tucked away in the corner with him.

And on March 24, Ian and God must've known how much I needed to hear from them. They must have known I'd been held underwater for as long as I could stay and still hold my breath.

I was sitting with Ian at the hospital, next to his luxury hospital bed underneath the rows of fluorescent lights. And all of a sudden . . .

"Ian, I'm going away for a few days," I had just said to him.

He reached for my hand.

I fluttered.

Did I see that? Does he know it's me?

I told him I needed to leave.

He reached for my hand again.

Ian, is that you? Is it really you?

I asked him to blink twice if he wanted me to stay longer.

He did.

I had never seen him blink so clearly.

Then, daringly, I asked him to blink twice if . . .

. . . if he loved me.

[Breathless pause.]

Blink.

Blink.

He did!

I didn't know how he dug himself out of his coma enough to show me, or why he'd done it this time and not any of the others. I didn't know what it meant for our future that he had lurched himself up out of the Vaseline and punched hard enough to move his eyes the way he needed to move them. I didn't know what it took to line up the neurons required to move his hand and convince my mind that he was coming back.

I'll never fully understand.

All I know is . . . it was perfect.

———————

Looking around our little suite now in the Murphys' house, the space originally built for Ian to come home to after the hospital, I see how much our world has shrunk so that we can fit into it.

We spent our first two years of marriage in a little ranch house after our wedding. Built in the '50s and sturdy like the people born in them, that was the first place we called home. Creating our first home had been such a blessing for me, because it was one part of our lives that I could somewhat control. The decorating, the colors, the mood it created. God frees us to create homes here that we love, where we feel comfortable, where we feel Him.

I'm thankful for our time in that little ranch house with the big yard and porch that created tons of memories with our friends and families. I'm grateful that Agnus, who lived there before us, planted beautiful flowers that still bloom, and put hooks all around the porch where I could string my lights and curtains. I'm thankful that our first two years together were spent there on that quiet little street, tucked in by pine trees. And I'm grateful it's but a mere shadow of what our home in heaven will feel like. Now we see in part.

Pulling in the driveway from our honeymoon, our families were waiting on the porch for us, joining us to open gifts. On that porch is where our dinner club was formed, underneath the re-used paper lanterns from my brother's wedding. We had all kinds of parties out there—the Kentucky Derby theme, the cowboy theme, the all-red theme. We watched movies and cooked big meals and squeezed fourteen people into a dining room built for six.

But we walked away from that home when we walked into writing a book, and the world we're in now seems much smaller. The distance from his side of the bed to the bathroom door takes just a few small steps, but they're steps that Ian is learning to take with the help of his walker. The medical equipment all has a spot, keeping at bay the sense of feeling overwhelmed. The power wheelchair, the loaner manual wheelchair that requires private pay, the Hoyer Lift and the shower chair all tell me that Ian isn't going to sling open the door and wrap me up into a hug anytime soon.

But this suite is home because so much of us was written inside these four walls. These were the walls that heard him say his name for the first time, and also the walls that welcomed him home from the hospital before he learned how to say his name again. And best of all, the familiar shadows of the sun setting over the patio umbrella just outside our window provides me a glimpse to a home that has no walls. The top of our down comforter that I can't bring myself to put away for summer reminds me of a God of rest.

As I look around and hear Ian's voice yelling the answers to his therapy from the dining room table—"Peter Piper picked!"—I see for a few fleeting seconds something beautiful and bigger than us. It's something we can't know yet, a secret tucked in between the years. But if I squint hard enough, I can see Jesus in front of the blind man, simultaneously addressing His disciples. I wait and ponder what my answer will be to His leading, searching question.

"Do you believe that I am able to do this?"

six

needed the exercise, so I decided to walk from my mom's house instead of driving. I was visiting a few weekends before Christmas, before enjoying my second Christmas as Ian's wife. Before I had left for the weekend, I reminded Ian of the things we had done in Christmases past, even before we were engaged.

"We made a lot of good Christmas memories, didn't we?" he asked.

He caught that glimpse I was sending to him, the glimpse that our life was full of good.

The walk felt good as the crisp country air swept into me. Seeing Ian unable to do most kinds of exercise that he liked before—running, basketball, baseball—was helping me to see that I needed to be moving as much as I could. If I wanted to take care of him after we'd both turned old, I needed to take care of myself before I even met thirty. And since I'd spent the morning baking Christmas cookies with my mom, I figured that I could shed both the guilt and plaque from my arteries by walking the half mile to my Grammy's house.

I couldn't come home without seeing her. She had taught me kindergarten, and whenever we helped her in the Blessing Shop (a thrift shop run by our church where she volunteered), she would buy us an éclair bar at Madge's, the small general store on the corner of our church parking lot. The shop was an old farmhouse, converted into rooms divided by clothing type, accessory, or size. The first room in the shop was the donation drop-off room. I remember spending what felt like hours digging through the garbage bags, sorting between men's jeans, children's clothes, ladies' dresses, etc. Sometimes I would personally help the customers, but mostly I sorted and hung the clothing. Sometimes I had money with me and could pick out a new hoodie or pair of Umbro soccer shorts.

On my walk to her trailer that day, I passed by my uncle's horses that were dressed for the new cold air, their strong backs tucked in underneath their black blankets, neighing their cold breath into the fresh air to greet me. The horses lived across the street from the farmhouse that I remember my aunt and uncle living in, a farm now run by a young flat-lander family—an adjective lovingly employed to describe folks that moved into our mountains from Philadelphia and New Jersey. Not having walked this portion of road for a few years, I noticed the old playhouse was gone, converted now into an outdoor wood stove and shed. It used to be our summer home when we spent our days at our uncle's farm, under the watch of our aunt. My mom had to go back to work when I was old enough to start having school days. That's why my Grammy taught me.

I made it to her house and she greeted me at the door, her tiny five-foot body slumping with age, but sporting a perfectly wrinkled ninety-year-old smile. Hugging me, she told me that she and her sister visiting from New York had just been sitting there, waiting for me to arrive.

Unlike the playhouse, everything in my Grammy's house was the same. The touch lamps on the couch ends, the thin gold living room carpet and the kitchen linoleum with the one visible spot where the handyman ran short on a piece and had to section it together. One of our games, growing up, was seeing who could find the double lines first on each visit.

I sat down in the rocking chair that had been my great-grandfather's. Other than a small squeak with each sway, it did well holding up my 130 pounds.

She sat down in her chair opposite me, a petite armless rocker, upholstered in soft pink. Her sister was sitting on the couch to my left, holding a cane, a new accessory. Conversation came quickly, as sunbeams popped through the lace curtains behind her.

"How's the book coming?" her second or third question wondered.

"Oh, it's coming."

"Maybe I shouldn't ask."

"No, you should ask. It's just a lot of work."

We circled my life for a few minutes, then shifted to hers and her sister's. My Grammy's arthritic hands clasped together and tucked themselves comfortably between her knees as she talked. The little gold diamond ring nestled in place by tightly wound thread facing her palm rested on her brown slacks.

"I wish I had known Grandpa Cecil," I said, breaking into a story Grammy was telling about the time she got a perm and Cecil wasn't impressed.

"He was a kind and loving and generous man," she managed to say. "We had a good life together."

Yes, they'd had a good twenty-four years together, planning for their twenty-fifth, when another heart attack became one too many. She wasn't with him when he had died. He had told her to go home, to finally leave the hospital for a little bit, to go check on the kids. She later felt as though he knew what was coming and just didn't want her there to see it.

A number of years later, however, she *did* see a husband die—the grandpa that I knew, her second husband—as she and this sister who was visiting her now sat one on each side of the nursing home bed. They held his hands as he fell into death, just as Lisa and I stepped into the room. I remember standing in the doorway, hearing my Grammy say his name in a way that seemed to know he was leaving. I remember seeing their backs hunch into their tears as they held his hands while the warmth of life trickled out.

"Every life has ups and downs," she spoke as she rocked. "You just have to make the best of it. You do what you have to do."

You do what you have to do.

Walking home after my visit, I looked out over the farmed meadow. Winter was coming, but the grass hadn't given up yet. Pockets of light green were embedded in the darker hue of fall grass and tall golden cornstalks, fighting to make their way up to beat the ensuing cold. The stalks were drying for harvest as their gold bodies obeyed the weight of the wind. Behind it all were bare, near-winter trees, so empty of leaves that they almost appeared black as the sunlight barely trickled through between the breaks and gaps and breaths.

But I knew that in just a few months, these black trees would be made new, saturated by spring's tender greens. I knew that deep inside of them, life was still brewing, still growing, still waiting for just the perfect time to appear.

"Please come soon," my breath fluttered, leaving my lips and entering alone into the brisk air, my little thrift store boots stepping me home.

———————

It was the beginning of April, and we were just waiting to bring him home, counting down the days on a little white board attached to his hospital closet door. Nothing felt better than the reward of changing those numbers, moving one day closer to Warren Road. We were telling him every time we visited what number he was on, even though he wasn't opening his eyes anymore. I could tell he was awake, just keeping his eyes shut. He was so clearly over it, so clearly trying to shut out the hospital as much as he could. And since he couldn't take himself out of the situation physically, he could at least close his eyes to it.

He also had an infection in one eye and spent too much time rubbing it. To keep him from irritating it and to keep the spasticity in his arms under control, the therapists made two hard-shell casts for him. We could take them off and on easily enough, but they restricted him from bending his arms.

So he had an eye constantly itching and two arms that couldn't reach it. He would fight hard against those casts, and I was just supposed to sit there and watch him struggle, to fight the natural rotation God created in the human shoulder. I wasn't supposed to take the casts off because his arms needed to be stretched, but I couldn't watch as he desperately tried to make his arms move. I couldn't watch him lie there, stuck in his bed, stuck in his mind, and consider it love. So I snuck them off whenever I thought I could get away with it, giving him the relief he needed, and then put them back before anyone noticed.

On April 14, my parents came to visit Ian and I, and brought him early birthday gifts. He actually had his eyes open that day. So I took off his casts and watched as he surprisingly reached his hand into the gift bag, removed the tissue paper, and pulled out the card and DVD. He pulled *everything* out, still staring straight ahead, as though a blinder was on his chin that kept him from seeing what his hands were doing. But we were thrilled at what we saw, because it was just another sign to us that there was life inside.

On April 16, Ian woke up to his twenty-second birthday in a hospital room, in the middle of Pittsburgh, without his family. He was actually awake that day, his eyes again open, as if he knew. I wanted his younger brothers to see him, so I offered to take them with me to the hospital, which meant I would only be able to stay for an hour or so, since their capacity for sitting in a hospital room was much lower than mine. But I had to take a guess that this would serve Ian better than having me there all day. I imagined it was the decision he would've made.

But leaving his room on his birthday after such a short visit left me with a full afternoon of guilt and anger. When we returned home from the trip, with so many hours remaining in Ian's first day of year twenty-two, I laid in my bed wondering if I'd made the right call. I could tell the guilt I was feeling was disproportionate to the situation, but I had no other way to process the sadness. And by the week after his birthday, I confessed for the first time into the pages of my journal that I was angry at Ian—angry that he had left me, and afraid that he had left me for good. I didn't know or understand why God was keeping him from me, why it was asking too much for me to get a little sympathy for what I was going through from the man I intended to spend forever with.

It was just such a confusing, emotional time. Because like any good screenplay, the end brings the beginning to life again. It brings it full circle. And with just five days to go until Ian was scheduled to come home, I couldn't think about it without crying. The ending I didn't want—Ian coming home with a severe disability—was reminding me of the beginning I had never asked for. We had been living in hospitals for seven months, listening to doctors for seven months, hoping to move the needle to normal life, even in the slightest, for seven months.

For seven long months . . .

———————

Ian was scheduled to come home on April 30. I had a job interview that day, which meant I couldn't ride home in the ambulance with him. I had first declined the interview for that very reason. I wanted to be there when he said goodbye to his therapists and doctors. I second-guessed myself, and then Steve second-guessed me. I called them back to accept.

But because I couldn't be there to ride home with him, I drove down the night before and stayed at the Heasley House. When I got into Ian's room that night, he was wide-awake.

When I came in the next morning to say goodbye and drive to my interview, he was wide-awake.

When Steve and Mary came that morning to put his clothes in bags and take him home, he was wide-awake.

He knew.

Even in his coma, he knew. Because comas didn't separate him from God.

He knew that he was going home to the house on Warren Road with the yellow siding and the backyard sized perfectly for a small baseball diamond. Eleven years of boyhood were waiting for him there with pencil marks on the doorway to the laundry room marking each brother's developing heights, year by year.

April 30, 2007
He's home:)

That's all we needed the blog post to say because the word *home* meant more than an ambulance ride from Pittsburgh. Ian grew up in a home that wasn't just layers of concrete and siding and shingles, but was a place of gathering. Mary made her home to bring comfort. So this new life at home meant being back to his parents and back to the kitchen where he used to eat breakfast in his boxers before class. It meant coming back to the Murphy smell, a smell that Ian would maybe now recognize because he'd been gone from it so long. A smell that every family possesses but is immune to its recognition.

Moving home for Ian meant a new bedroom on the back of the house on the first floor, below the other bedrooms. It had thin slats of Pergo instead of well-worn brown carpet like his old bedroom. His new walls were of the same Celtic Folklore green paint chip as the living room. Ian always commented on how relaxed he felt in the living room, and Mary wanted him to feel the same way now. His new room had lamps and a mirror and blinds that Mary had picked out to make the room feel masculine, like a place where a man would want to recover. And temporarily, thanks to our friend Vikki who snuck over before the ambulance arrived, Ian's room was also filled with a full constellation of welcome-home balloons. She knew we were on our way to celebrate.

Then . . . Ian was home.

He came inside the lower level of his house, into the kitchen and dining room and living room and den. He didn't need to go upstairs because we'd brought everything down to him. He had everything he needed.

He was home.

It was a warm day, and there was a new patio courtesy of Ian's addition, so that's where we spent our first evening. Being home meant Ian could go outside whenever we felt he should. Plus, his new room had six big windows, allowing him (unlike at the hospital) to fall asleep with the breeze brushing over his worn-out body.

On May 1, 2007, after 212 mornings waking up alone in a hospital room, Ian woke up covered in home-washed sheets under the humming of his ceiling fan. He woke up one story away from his family. He woke up one story away from his three-year-old sister who couldn't see a disability but *could* see her brother. He woke up one story away from a lifetime surrounded with people that just wanted to love him.

He woke up . . . home.

———

"Look! Lights!" Clara gasps as she rides on Ian's lap, calling to me and pointing at the few houses on the alley that are decorated for Christmas.

We turn toward the houses and stop to look at each one. Her little body is wrapped under her uncle's arm and her pink blankie, which is only big enough to reach down to

Ian's knees and up over her chest. I slowly push the wheel-chair forward to the lights because I don't want to go back. I don't want Ian to say goodbye to this moment.

Pretending to be a little family unit, I give Clara and Paladin a bath after dinner. Uncle Ian tells them a story, about a girl in the circus with a pink tutu named Larissa and her boyfriend Leonard, who rode a motorcycle to the circus and proposed with a plastic bag full of flowers and dirt. We lie underneath the Christmas tree on a soft blanket pulled down from the couch. They each sit with their blankies, miniature mugs of tea and a cookie, all bundled up to watch Rudolph.

I pause and look at them—babies around and a dish-washer full and the floor swept clean. Uncle Ian kisses them goodnight and I, Aunt Rara, carry them upstairs.

I walk back down the carpeted steps and see my husband sitting underneath the lights of the tree after I've put the babies to bed. I look at him, and for a moment I see why he needed to keep going and not die in the hospital. I see why, after six years, it was worth every pill dose, every therapist prompt, every transition into a shower chair. Ian had life before him. He had nieces and nephews who needed to love him. He had brothers and sisters-in-law who needed to see God through a shattered knee and catheter bag.

He had a girlfriend he needed to make his wife, because she needed to learn to love.

seven

Coming home for Ian meant we could almost have a normal life again—normal, because we could go places, but not that we fit in normally when we did. I often wondered what we looked like from the outside. I remember one day before we came home, still at the hospital, seeing a patient who appeared to have a similar injury as Ian's. I saw some of her family with her and was overwhelmed with pity for them. Then I realized that I was the same as them; I just couldn't see it as clearly in ourselves.

I even thought that sometimes it might've been sadder looking at us from the outside than it did from inside, sadder for people who only knew the brain-injured Ian—because to me, the man I fell in love with was still very much alive in there. When I'd push him in his chair or watch him in therapy, I was with the same person who'd asked me on our first date the previous November. I didn't always see the wheelchair. I saw my boyfriend, then my fiancé, then my husband.

But one thing I could never imagine was what his body felt and knew and understood being in the hospital for seven months. Even on week-long vacations, I usually ache toward the end to go home and become entrenched again in the familiar walls. His body, too, must have known that it was someplace foreign. And so coming home meant he got to wake up. To change back. To return.

To something resembling normal.

And it was often so exciting.

Consistently he started reaching for my hand to hold it and was showing me in other ways that he was listening, interacting, and wanting me close. For instance, I was reading my Bible in his room a few days after he came home and couldn't remember how to pronounce the word "Babel." I pronounced it one way and asked him if I was right. He blinked to say "no." I said it a different way and asked him again. He blinked to say "yes." I repeated the right pronunciation a few times to validate his answer . . . because if I was going to explode about it to his parents or on the blog, I wanted to make sure I'd interpreted it right.

He was also starting to smile again—something I hadn't seen him do since a smile had randomly escaped his lips while we were at the first rehab unit. It had probably been gas, but I wanted to believe it was a smile, and that he was smiling because I was standing next to him. On this day at home in May, however, there was no doubt. He smiled several times.

He was coming back to me.

But even though he was smiling and reaching for my hand, the feeling of being in his home where we used to stay up late talking and flirting and where we had our first meal with his family meant I was becoming enveloped in a new sense of loss. It felt impossible to be content for more than just a few seconds with the little steps he was making, because I was constantly surrounded by things that reminded me of the twenty-one years before the accident. And I'm human, so hope doesn't always come easily. I wrestled for contentment in my young heart, hoping that God could change Ian's situation, yet wanting to have hope that even if He didn't, we would still be okay.

Sometimes the deepest struggles came in the most unexpected places. Although I was living with Ian's family, I didn't have anything to do with his medical care. We had several daily shifts of caregivers, and Mary and Steve wanted to protect me from being responsible for that. They also wanted to preserve Ian's dignity. After all, I was still just his girlfriend. They wanted me to be a relief for Ian, a person who was dedicated solely to having fun with him. And I appreciated that.

But it also meant I didn't get to see Ian a ton, because I'd started a new part-time job and because his day was busy with showering and therapy and stretching and also with needing to sleep a lot more, giving his brain time to rest. Many evenings he was asleep after we'd all sat around the dinner table.

My heart just didn't know what to do with caregivers and parents who were responsible for caring for Ian's every need. I didn't want him to be home and limited and unable to go to the bathroom on his own. I didn't want someone else to be washing him in the shower or calculating how many bowel movements he had in a day. All of those things happened in the hospital, but when they happened in the home I was living in, it was totally different. I didn't want him to be so sick that a parent or caregiver had to be in the house with him at all times. I didn't like it that if the house caught on fire, I wouldn't know how or be able to get Ian out by myself. I couldn't bear the thought of someone else taking care of Ian.

Because normal life wasn't like that.

I stayed up too late on most days, just because I wanted to say good night to him. He would shower and stretch at night, which meant that sometimes I couldn't go in his room to pray for him until much past the time when I should have gone to bed. Long into the evening, all I could usually see of Ian was the closed, locked barrier of his bedroom door.

For years, this stirred something ugly inside of me. Something about the closed door made me feel so angry and useless. It was a beautiful oak door our friend Susan had taken to her house to stain when the addition was being built. I remember how much Mary loved how it looked when Susan brought it back, because it matched perfectly with the floors and trim. But when that door was shut and locked, it meant something was happening in the room that I couldn't be a part of . . . because I wasn't Ian's wife. If he needed to go to the bathroom or if his catheter leaked, there was nothing I could do. And I felt helpless.

That closed door made me fly to my knees on so many nights, crouching in my room as Lydia slept in the bed next to me, asking God to have mercy on me. I hated knocking on the door and hearing someone yell "Don't come in!" because it meant if I had somehow walked in accidentally, I would see something that would mortify Ian, and would mortify me, because he didn't yet own my body, nor I his, because we weren't yet married.

Fortunately my nighttime sadness was usually inter-rupted by my miniature roommate. Lydia got up a lot, usu-ally making her way into Steve and Mary's room despite my half-awake attempts to dissuade her.

"Mama?" she'd ask when she arrived at Mary's bedside.

"What do you need, Lydia?"

"My lips are chapped. I need ChapStick."

Mary would stumble her way back to our bedroom as I pretended to be asleep, not wanting to make her feel the need to talk with me in her stupor.

"Where is it, sweetie?"

"It's on my bed stand."

"Well, honey, why did you come wake me up if it was right by your bed?"

"I couldn't reach it"—which was technically true. She couldn't have reached it without shifting her weight in bed. Perhaps, though, she'd made a better choice by not trying, because shifting her weight on those hot pink satin sheets could propel her right onto the floor.

Jan had given these sheets to her as a Christmas present. "This is going to be hilarious," I said, after Lydia had opened them. "She's going to slip right out of bed using those." And she certainly did, that very night. I bolted out of bed, only to find her still sound asleep on the floor, crumpled in the perfect position for me to lift her up and set her back onto the mattress.

So watching Lydia and enjoying her antics was one way I passed the time. I also did my best to get to know Ian's brothers, their young ages keeping us from naturally ending up in the same environments. I pretended to like the Steelers, just as I had done with Ian. We had worn matching shirts to the Super Bowl party in 2006. I tried to act like I'd grown up watching football, when actually my high school wasn't even big enough to field a team. Our homecoming games were soccer, which was good news for me, since I was the left fullback. Sundays at the Whiteley house growing up were for falling asleep to a NASCAR race, not spent on the den couch clad in football jerseys and staring straight ahead at the television, right next to their siblings, the way the Murphy men did.

Around Ian's brothers, I made a point of being the big brother's annoying girlfriend, commenting on the color of the team's pants or the logos on the helmets. Not because it was the only thing I noticed, but because it fit the stereotype and I wasn't about to pretend I knew what "clipping" or "handoffs" meant. Still the boys welcomed me into the den as long as I didn't interrupt too much and as long as I held my questions until the commercials—a rule they still try to hold today now that they have wives equally as uninterested, but who don't want to stay away from their men for four hours straight on the weekend.

So I passed the time just being together with the Murphys, listening to podcasts, watching movies, and looking to the boys and Lydia for distractions, holding gently the social plans and other expectations that must be adjusted and flexible, not white-knuckled, when health is not a guarantee. Being in a house filled with life helped me make it through.

But people still worried about me at times.

"You need something to keep you going," Steve said to me one day as he leaned against the kitchen countertop. "Mary has Lydia and the boys and the antique shop. You don't have anything."

Laughter fills me now as I recall it, because I knew he was trying to convey love. But in that moment, his comment stung. It only sounded degrading to me, because the words he chose—"You don't have anything"—made me feel as though I had nothing to be living for outside of an improved Ian.

What he meant, and what his wife clarified for me later in her soft and gentle way, was that the spaces in my brain that used to be filled with learning how to write news releases in college or put notes from sheet music onto piano keys needed to be stimulated. I needed to fill my mind with something other than sitting by a bed—not as a *replacement* for that responsibility, but just as a *diversion*. Steve and Mary knew why I was staying. They were the biggest advocates for me to keep loving Ian. But they also knew that one way I could serve Ian well was by taking care of myself.

So I hauled myself to the gym, trusting in the science of endorphins to keep me moving forward. And it helped. I worked to establish a habit, because habits are hard to break. And *this* habit—the habit of moving my body and making it stronger—was a habit that could help me later as Ian's wife. I wanted my body to be able to take care of him. And even though I didn't have the strong, masculine frame his brothers did, I knew God could strengthen my bones to take care of him.

I wanted to move my body because Ian couldn't move his own. And so I prayed my way through aerobics classes and crunches, begging God to let Ian once again feel the strength that moves through bodies in motion.

I also wanted to move my body as good stewardship of my youthful years. As Ian and I grow old together, even as the varicose veins pop through my skin along with the wrinkles, I want to be thankful for all I'd done with the time when strength development came more easily, when endurance locks into place and follows you into life.

I wanted to be there for Ian.

I wanted to be there a long time.

And what I didn't see in those lonely days, those moments of despair, was that God was emptying a space in my heart, refilling it with Himself, letting me see Him in the small moments of joy. Because only a great God could bring joy into a brain injury.

I started packing my bags for Florida, set to go on a get-away trip with Jan. Looking for a laptop case, I found Ian's old one in his old bedroom, the zipper having aged much faster because of the amount of time it had spent unused. I searched through the pockets to make sure everything was out of it before filling it with my own things for keeping me occupied on the plane.

Reaching my hand inside the front pocket, I felt small sheets of paper, neatly folded and tucked into envelopes. Pulling them out one by one, I saw they were letters I had sent to Ian from my Pittsburgh apartment, where I'd lived while doing my internship at the Red Cross while he made the film. Each one had landed in his Marietta Avenue mailbox and had been brought inside by Mr. Hamilton, the owner of the house he was staying in, an older gentleman, widowed, who spent his days gardening and teaching violin lessons. Photos were tucked into the pockets as well—photos I had sent him throughout the summer, so that while he was selling his soul to movie production he wouldn't forget what I looked like.

Florida, meant to be a distraction and post-college cel-ebration for Jan and I, brought its own relief but also sad-ness, ebbing in and out with the tide. The saltwater breezes calmed my fried emotions, but the physical distance I'd placed between myself and Ian brought fear and cautious-ness that maybe I wasn't really ready to be a thousand miles from his bedside. Still, laughter came easily with Jan, a var-ied benefit from having such a rare find in a friend.

One night, lame pick-up lines entered our conversation as we mocked the worst. "Hey, my boyfriend's in a coma.

Wanna go out?" I mimicked, clumsily spewing forth the words in silly, punchy carelessness.

I think I intended it to be a joke. But out with the words came a gush of terror that my life had actually unfolded into this. How for one second could my heart think this was funny?

Jan looked at me, and I knew she felt my emptiness. I had suddenly glimpsed where despondency could take me. I could easily deceive myself into being unfaithful or disrespectful of Ian unless I could fight against the pull of my emotions. I desperately loved the man who was lying comatose and unmoving in a bed. But the fact that I could toss jokes about him meant I was capable of choosing a life I did not wish to have.

My comment lingered in the air for a few minutes until Jan and I awkwardly walked along the edge of the dock that had been pieced together with rough and unfinished boards. We distracted ourselves with taking weird photos and made up a story about what a great job she'd done in picking out the yacht that was in front of us. I joked my way back into normal conversation, but my heart was aching all night. And lying on my pillow, I silently cried in the dark as Jan slept nearby. Life was too real. And sometimes its reality was shocking to me.

On our plane ride home, I imagined what would happen if Ian had "woken up" while I was gone. I could almost see him sitting on the patio in his jeans and Goodwill T-shirt, just waiting for me. I wanted to be greeted and hugged and told that I was missed and asked to tell every single detail of the last week.

Instead I sat by his bed and watched his coma.

I knew he was working hard to get better for me. Yet he couldn't fight against his body enough to stay awake.

Coming home to him was obviously better than coming home to an empty room and a memory. But my expectations weren't happening fast enough for me, and I didn't know if Ian could ever get healthy enough to make me feel any different about everything.

Soon after Florida, I took another trip with Jan and a few friends to a conference in Kentucky. The week before the trip, I was still telling Ian that he needed to come with me, still convincing myself he could be up and out of his bed by then. He *had* to go, I thought, because it was at this conference the year before that I'd finally decided I didn't want anyone else but him.

We had been apart from each other on our internships for a few weeks, and God had removed all fear and doubt from my heart about Ian as I sat in the van with the other young twenty-somethings on our way to The Galt House Hotel. I had been afraid to truly say yes to him, yes to wanting him for the rest of my life. Fear had snuck in, telling me I would probably fall out of love with him someday, which meant it wasn't worth all the hard work and heartache. The fear was sneaking lies to me, whispering them to me, tricking me into thinking that my own ability to create love was greater than God's.

But somehow truth broke into the van and into my journal as I scribbled along. I didn't want to be scared that he would find someone better or someone he could enjoy more, or that he would realize I was actually a really boring person.

We reconciled at the conference that year, in a classy food court fit for young love drama. I shared my heart with him, and I was ready to fully commit and was ready not to be scared. It became a sweet three days as I felt a newness of him—exciting, because I got to see Ian differently and imagine a real future with him.

The city where we stayed had horse-drawn carriage rides you could take through the center of town. I've always loved horses, or loved the thought of horses—from a distance. Ian took me on one of those carriage rides, passing by all of his friends as they walked back and forth from the conference center to their hotels, willing to daringly show them a very visible expression of his love for this young college student. But he did it because he loved me.

Going to the conference the year *after* Ian's accident, however—*without* him—meant I had to face all those memories again. I had to face them without Ian, and without Ian even realizing I was back there.

The next morning, before Jan and Arwen and Bethany picked me up, I cried because Ian didn't have the chance to come with me and because he couldn't even get himself out of bed. I cried because it wasn't fair that I could have this experience, this time away, and he couldn't. He had been so active the year before. And now, those abilities that made him so vocal and influential had been stripped from him. I wanted wholeness for him. I wanted those seven months of not giving up in the hospital to mean something, to come back to him.

"Rebekah, I want you to have this notecard I found in his Bible," I told Ian's cousin from New Orleans as I met her outside during a break. It was well-worn, folded in between the pages of his Bible with the peeling cover, written in the cherished font of his own chicken scratch.

Whom have I in heaven but you? And there is nothing on earth that I desire besides you. My flesh

and my heart may fail, but God is the strength of
my heart and my portion forever. (Psalm 73:25–26)

She framed the card when she got home, the text protected from wear by glass, reminding her.

Meanwhile, his Bible kept me company as I attended the
various sessions, getting suffocated under my grip when I
started seeing people who'd ask questions about him—people who only knew me because of my relationship with him.

"How's Ian doing?"

"We've been praying for you so much."

"We're so encouraged by Ian's story. We have so much
faith that God will continue to heal."

I felt assaulted by raw grief, wanting to receive these
glimpses of hope, yet feeling enveloped by my sadness,
barely able to respond through my pasted-on smile to the
love I was being shown. And so after the sessions ended,
instead of going to a late-night concert or hanging out somewhere, grief pushed me to bed. I could only hold these conversations for so long, and I could only pretend to be okay
for so long. Deep down, I had joy and knew that God loved
us. But that didn't change how raw the loss was.

And that's when I began to realize: I really shouldn't
be there. I had signed up for this conference because somewhere in my head, not going meant avoiding. Not going
meant not loving and trusting God enough to show others
an appropriately Christian response to suffering. I felt like
I needed to keep doing these normal things because, well,
maybe they would make me feel normal again. And maybe
someone would see me and be amazed by a God who could
sustain me through this.

But what I didn't know—and wouldn't allow myself to accept—was that I could insert myself into my grief and pull back from things that maybe were just a little too much.

We had already chosen to make our story public by sharing the details on the blog and making ourselves vulnerable, Steve and I. We knew things were happening because of it, that God was doing things we couldn't see. Yet then, and now, I didn't realize that God wasn't using our lives at the cost of His personal ministry to us. Gently, even as my father here would do, He was providing care to us—to me—and I was just overlooking it.

"If one person is saved, if one marriage is saved, this will all be worth it." That was our mantra. We knew it and believed it. Even Devon, Ian's little brother, made Jesus part of his life in the hospital as he watched his brother die, so we knew God was truly working.

Yet I let myself focus on the giving up, the sacrificing, and didn't see that God was caring for me as well. He had storehouses of riches at His feet if only I would see them, if only I would reach out and touch His garment. He wasn't asking me to keep giving and giving and choosing the uncomfortable life of vulnerability without prefacing it with grace. Like in my decision to go to the conference, I was pushing hard to do what I felt was expected of me by man, but not by God.

And God was the only one who was going to get me through this.

———

With a brain injury, the patient is still alive but they're different. When a person dies, of course, as a believer, their death is immediately swallowed up into Christ. We can understand that—as much as *any* human can understand it—and the awareness of its truth gives us closure. We know that his or her soul is now in the heavenly place it was created by God to be. But with Ian, I didn't have that same kind of closure. Instead, I spent days wondering where that Ian was, the Ian I fell in love with. I wondered what part of his brain was taken out that made him throw his head back and hold his belly as he laughed. I wondered what neurological pathway enabled him to walk, and where that pathway went, and how it could possibly be of use anywhere else but back in Ian's brain.

Then one day, amid the slow plodding of his recovery and the endless pondering of my heart, a glimmer of hope returned.

Ian hugged me for the first time in eight months.

I had given him hugs before, but not all-around hugs, not the kind of hug that means something. There was always a bed pillow or wheelchair seat in the way that kept my arms from encircling him. I couldn't get them all the way around him, just around his shoulders and neck.

Steve had made a therapy table for Ian to use, and we kept it in the corner of his room. It was covered with thick matting to make it soft, but it was harder than a mattress. He also rigged up a system with PVC pipes so that Ian would have a railing to hold onto. His trunk control was still really weak, and so he needed to practice sitting up. Our caregiver and Steve would work together with Ian each night, directing his hand to the railing and helping him straighten himself whenever he'd start to lean to one side. His body had atrophied a little after all those days in the hospital, so he needed to relearn how to make his mind hold up his weight. At that point, we were celebrating him being able to balance himself, sitting up, holding onto the railing with one hand. For thirty seconds.

One Saturday—the ninth of June—I came into the room just before he was finishing up his time on the mat, and I asked Steve if I could try to hug Ian.

I stepped toward him and knelt down. And as soon as I did, he reached his right arm to my left wrist and traced my skin up to my shoulder. He curved his arm around the curve of my back until I was comfortably pulled into him. He shifted his head into the curve where my shoulder met my neck. It seemed like his instinct. It seemed like he knew exactly what he was doing. And in that moment, a tingle of excitement buzzed through my heart that I'd almost forgotten how to feel.

From then on, I waited every night for my hug. After he had worked hard at his sitting-up exercises, and just before he went back to bed, they would call me in to hug him. I cancelled plans and rearranged schedules, just so I could be there and not miss my chance to feel his affection again.

Pretty soon, he was reaching across his body to hold my hand any time I was next to him. One day the physical therapist was trying to get him to give her a high five, but he just wouldn't do it. Finally, in exasperation, she called for me to come in, and I asked Ian to hold my hand. He did it. Three times. The therapist was crying because she'd been asking Ian to do that for three weeks.

Yes, even in his silent, distant condition, Ian kept reaching for me, touching my face. With his blinks, he would tell me he loved me. With his hugs, he would tell me he cared for me. God was giving us these moments, moments of refreshment in each other, moments of experiencing love, carved into the midst of days when love had felt so absent.

Ian was showing me, without words, how much I meant to him.

———————

It was our third Valentine's Day as spouses, and the first day in a while when I felt really happy in him and in our marriage. I couldn't keep a straight face looking at him, rubbing his bare shoulders before we gave in to sleep for the night, and I made him look me in the eyes like he used to do when we were dating.

"I'm so happy, Ian. I'm actually happy tonight. Can you imagine what heaven must feel like when we're released into complete and perfect joy?"

"I can't wait to share that with you."

I stopped, a smile peering out of my lips. He loves me so much that he's looking forward to sharing heaven's greatest joys *with me*. He's excited for us to see each other in perfection as we come into Christ and into the fullness He has promised us. He wants that for me. He wants it so much for me that he pushes me toward that.

This is deeper love than I offer him in return. Yet that does not stop him.

———————

On June 21, 2007, Ian had a test to see if he could swallow thickened liquids. He did great, which meant that in addition to getting food through his stomach tube, he could now start making steps toward eating through his mouth again. To celebrate, we gave him a cup of coffee, something he'd been without for nine months.

A few days after the swallowing test, he sat in a "normal" chair for the first time, a wingback chair in his room. We had to use the Hoyer Lift to get him into it, but it was so exciting to see him in something non-medical—no seat belt like on his wheelchair, no straps around his chest like they used in therapy to keep him upright. It was just Ian. Sitting.

And it was wonderful.

He also started shaking and nodding his head to communicate with us, instead of using blinks, which was huge. It gave us so much more clarity into his wants and desires. Steve was shocked the first time he saw it because, while he had heard our reports, he hadn't seen it in person. As Steve was helping Ian into bed one night, he asked Ian if he wanted a pillow, and Ian clearly shook to indicate "no." We were watching Ian change, and praising God for even the seemingly small things. As Steve noted on our blog, "It's good to come home from work, sit down next to him in his wheelchair, and have him turn his head toward me and look right at me. When I think about where he was, it really is amazing to see his progress."

But as Ian started making strides like these—drinking fluids and sitting up more easily, nodding his head for "yes," shaking his head for "no"—he also started showing signs that he was discouraged. His therapists and doctors told us this was normal—that as most patients wake up, they start to realize their disabilities, which creates a new group of struggles for them to work through. Many patients battle depression as the fog lifts from their coma, revealing to them a disabled body underneath.

And I couldn't seem to keep it from discouraging me too. I felt useless again because I couldn't promise Ian a release from his struggles or take them away myself. I could *pray* for him, but sometimes that didn't feel like enough. It didn't offer him a visible or tangible change.

Ian was living so close to the surface of his coma, so close to being able to talk to us. We were all waiting and hoping that soon he would come back. And while waiting, we know, is a good thing—like the nine-month anticipation God creates inside the womb—the living of it is long and impatient. We were each being forced to learn that it's inside the womb of waiting where beauty and character grows.

The late summer and early fall of 2007 was so different from those of past years in the Murphy lore, thanks to that life-shattering event from the previous September. But undaunted, the time rolled around for the annual family vacation to the lake in Virginia. And come what may, they were going.

With Ian.

It was the first year in his full allotment of twenty-two that he wouldn't be able to get in the water with his cousins or stay up late watching movies. But we hoped the sights and sounds of this every-year celebration would be a boost to his system.

This would be only my second year to visit the lake house myself. And thinking about going with this version of Ian, rather than the one I'd enjoyed so hilariously and wholeheartedly the year before, wasn't a thought I liked to keep in my mind. But thinking about *not* going was even worse. I just hoped we could pull it off. And if we did, I hoped everybody could experience at least a little of what made this anticipated event so special.

An understatement, of course, to say that this was a production. We packed Ian's bed, his Hoyer Lift, and tons of medical supplies. Steve went ahead to the house before us and built a ramp to get Ian inside. And even though it was difficult to take care of Ian in a new environment not made for wheelchairs and feeding tube poles, it was a place that held memories so valuable to Ian, the payoff was worth the work. Ian's cousins were able to spend time just talking to him and keeping him company. We were all able to laugh together and enjoy the company that Ian had always looked forward to. He loved the two weeks at the lake.

And I loved the family spirit that wouldn't deny it for him.

Upon our return, Ian spent the rest of the summer fighting thrush, a yeast-based infection that had crept into his throat and mouth. It made swallowing incredibly painful, meaning the progress he had made in learning how to swallow foods like applesauce and pudding was slowing down.

At that point in his health progression, discomfort usually led him to respond with sleep, or at least with *pretending* to be asleep—because if his eyes were closed, no one would try to make conversation or ask things of him. Often I would find him in his bed with his eyes closed, not really asleep but seemingly trying to escape or find rest. It was sad to see him trying to compensate for pain, yet having no means to adjust his situation himself.

But still, he kept battling—like the day Steve noticed him pointing to his stomach, then realized that Ian was two hours past his normal lunchtime. And yet nothing quite prepared us for what we discovered on September 17.

Ian could read.

The organization of his brain had been tossed around like the inside of a snow globe, the way a small child twists and revolves the crystals in the glass, but his language skills were still intact. This discovery, this erasing of fears, was a small key for unlocking and revealing the Ian that we'd believed was still in there the whole time. Knowing he could read meant his mind was still *his* mind, that it hadn't reverted back to that of a five-year-old, which was often my fear. Knowing he could read meant we could develop an entirely new system of communicating with him instead of using calculated blinks and yes-or-no questions. Knowing he could read meant the man we'd been praying for, who lived underneath that coma, was not just a figment of our hopeful imagination.

Maybe marriage wasn't so far away.

The therapists built a little board where we could clip sheets of paper containing answers for questions that Ian would know. Like putting up both my name and Lydia's name, and then asking him to point to his sister's name. Or putting up the name of two sitcoms, and then giving him character names to identify which show they came from.

We had been taught about brain plasticity at the ICU. Brain plasticity means that even though pathways are destroyed, the brain has a way of rerouting itself, compensating and rebuilding so that things once lost can return. The healthy parts of the brain surrounding the damaged ones are able to pick up the slack, taking on responsibilities and processes that hadn't been their job before. I didn't know for sure if that's how it really worked. The topic had garnered a lot of available research. And the doctors who explained it to us were, thankfully, trying to give us hope that Ian could regain what we sometimes thought was hopeless. Simply knowing the term and the potential it offered was enough for me.

A few days later, I tried an experiment to make this more personal. I put up two restaurant names. Then I asked him which one he took me to on our first date.

He got it right.

So the memory of that night was still in there, I convinced myself. Or maybe if it wasn't in there, he at least knew enough about himself to deduce which restaurant was more likely to be his choice for a special night. Either way, I took the answer. God had again shown us that He was watching.

———

We very soon approached the one-year anniversary of that horrible Saturday, when screeching tires and phone calls and taps on the shoulder and shocked expressions transformed all our lives into a horror film we couldn't turn off. I prayed my way through those days, sitting by Ian's bed and watching him sleep. I prayed as my hands massaged the deep crevices on his skull where bone flaps had been removed, both to relieve pressure from the swelling as well as to take out the parts of his brain that didn't work anymore. I felt the bump on his scalp from the shunt they'd installed and followed the trail of the tube down the inside of his neck, the tube that made a fake vein from below his ear into his chest.

It was all so . . . unreal. Even then.

Watching him lie in bed with the metal railings lifted to prevent him from falling, I admit I sometimes questioned why God had spared him in that car. Death—or, I mean, the relief he would've experienced in death—occasionally seemed better to me than a brain injury. Because more than I wanted to be his wife someday, I wanted him to feel release. To step from underneath the brown ceiling fan and out onto the cloak of God's garment in heaven. And if God could see that the only thing separating Ian from completion with Him in heaven was a breath, surely He would not withhold that from His child.

But God was still God, of course, which I was not. And He was obviously keeping heaven from Ian because of something. God knew (as He would slowly begin revealing to us) that this was not the end. One day Ian would feel life pour through his arms and trickle into his unused ankles. God knew that He Himself would rush through Ian's veins, the strength and completeness layering itself around, doubling over and out of his body.

What peace, I often thought, would seep into my marrow—grief and sorrow, yes, but peace—if Ian could be released from this body, removed, carried, all of his years swarming into a blink, a shutter, as the lashes close and fold. Peace would follow the escape from brokenness as he finally gained wholeness and departed his weakness.

Yet God was keeping him. And we were praying. Praying for God's will, for both healing *and* for heaven. Still, God kept him for what must have been purposes unknown— because even though I could see them sometimes, the purposes didn't outweigh the heaviness of missing my Ian and watching him live in limbo.

Why then are we here? Would God keep His children out of paradise a single moment longer than was necessary? Why is the army of the living God still on the battlefield when one charge might give them the victory? Why are His children still wandering hither and thither through a maze, when a solitary word from His lips would bring them into the centre of their hopes in heaven? The answer is— they are here that they may "live unto the Lord," and may bring others to know His love. We remain on earth as sowers to scatter good seed; as ploughmen to break up the fallow ground; as heralds publishing salvation. We are here as the "salt of the earth," to be a blessing to the world.—Charles Spurgeon, *Morning and Evening*

eight

watched as autumn drifted into the ugliness of October, the grass only green in small patches, the rest merging into brown or yellow. All the leaves had fallen from the trees, leaving bare brown outlines against the sky. Soon those outlines would be covered in white, and even though I hated the cold, I loved the view of fresh snow.

It was the same with our lives too. Life had seemed to be going along so beautifully. On September 29, 2006, I had spent the evening with Ian's family and his grandparents. On September 30, life moved into the hospital, and we abruptly started living an existence that wasn't so pretty anymore— or, at least, it required more discovery.

I couldn't wait for it to be over. But this wasn't all there was. God had many promises still coming to us. One day, I believed, our lives would seem beautiful again. One day this season of sadness would be over. "I believe," said the writer of Psalm 27:13, "that I shall look upon the goodness of the LORD in the land of the living!"

But what would our living look like in Year Two?

———————

Adjusting to caregivers in our life and the need for others' opinions and counsel in Ian's care is a struggle I still haven't completely overcome, even today. But in Year Two, I could tell I was battling with anger at this reality and the intrusion it brought into my relationship with Ian. I didn't know what to do with my anger, or with how it was affecting those closest to me.

I was so angry that Ian couldn't make decisions for himself, which meant we all had to make our own assumptions. But I was angry when people assumed they knew what was going on in Ian's heart better than I did. I was angry when people assumed, for example, that he wanted to spend four hours at a time in his room without distractions or company. Including, of course, me.

Sure, assumptions were basically all we could go on. And we all in part projected onto him what we wanted for ourselves. But I just wanted to be with Ian. And this desire made me assume that I would've always been his first choice as well.

Before the accident, Ian had a way of melting my anger into laughter, a rare skill that came with his sense of humor, which was a package deal when dating him. Even times when I was angry at him, he could just look at me with a certain set of eyes or gesticulate his body a certain way, and it morphed the hardness of my heart. I could barely even employ *fake* anger with him because he saw right through it and knew exactly what to do to make me laugh.

But during these awkward silent years, when he had no voice or facial expressions or control of his body, he couldn't make me laugh. I could sit by his bed and tell him what I was struggling with, but I usually told it to resting eyes. I usually told it to a man who was giving all he could give just to stay awake for a few minutes at a time, sometimes one or two hours between naps. I could confess my sins aloud in his presence, but even though God wasn't sleeping, my helper was silent.

And so there I sat with my anger next to a silent man in a bed. And the loss was oozing into me so deeply that even those struggles of mine that were totally unrelated to Ian wielded the power to unravel me, one sad day without him at a time.

> *October 16, 2007*
> I'm officially the most mean-spirited, sinful person in the world. No matter what I do, love, it is covered with sin. But so often, instead of this causing me to cling tighter to the cross, I just feel overwhelmed. I hate everything about this trial and the sin that it causes me to face. Yet obviously God has me here because I needed to be sanctified in these areas. I wish that I had just a sweet countenance that always expected the best of people and always assumed the best of them. Instead, I do the complete opposite! And I am always seeking myself above all else.

I was in despair (a still familiar visitor) that God had given the wrong person to Ian. Surely someone with a gentler decorum and demeanor could summon up a better response to this trial than I was doing. If I had a more tender heart, I could take care of Ian better and not get so angry at our caregivers or Ian's parents, simply because they were doing something I wasn't able to do. If I was only more gentle and quiet, then Ian would be a better man.

If I could somehow transform myself into Jane Bennett, and treat Ian as she treated Mr. Bingley, then all would be so much better, even here in my non-Victorian world, or at least in Ian's world. Jane Austen had created Jane into a calm, not-so-spunky character who could endure difficulty without getting sassy. She had a quiet but strong manner, as opposed to her sister Lizzy. Those two so often resembled myself and my own sister Lisa who, as the eldest, was ever calm, was only spanked once in her life (which happened to be totally undeserved anyway), and never caused my parents any heartburn while she was in college.

I, on the other hand, did.

Often.

And I couldn't control my sass.

"You can dish it out, but you can't take it," I heard over and over from my family growing up, particularly from my brother.

"You always need to have the last word."

"You like arguing so much, you should be a lawyer. Even your initials spell LAW."

"Can you please stop biting my head off as soon as you wake up in the morning?"

I guess I was born with it, the ability to stand up for myself, whether right or wrong, and the need to speak my opinion—again, whether right or wrong. Most often wrong. Like in high school, when I wrote a letter to the editor of the newspaper because there was talk of furloughing our Spanish teacher, which would mean just one foreign language teacher for the entire school. Or the time we all got in trouble on our senior class trip, and after returning I informed the principal of some double standards that were being upheld, which ultimately helped my fellow classmates and me tremendously in our efforts to establish innocence and be able to participate in our graduation ceremony.

The causes I usually fought for, however, weren't even close to being noble, and often only got me into trouble, not because I wanted to be a bad kid but because I simply wanted "justice," which is interpreted much differently by a fourteen-year-old than by her parents.

Yet meanwhile, little did I know, across the grand state of Pennsylvania, a little Ian Murphy was also sassing his way through life with sarcasm and wit, equally bad morning attitudes, and a will stronger than the two legs that carried him. More self-aware than I, he would at least return to his mom later in the day and repent. "Was I rude this morning? I don't even remember talking, but was I rude?"

Ian's and Larissa's scenes in our respective home movies from childhood were eerily similar, though filmed so far away geographically and separate in all other ways. To edit video clips of us together would make someone think we were twins separated at birth, born a month and two hundred miles apart, because we each spent the majority of the time jumping up and down in front of the camera, begging for attention.

Ian's cinematic efforts eventually became much more refined than mine, turning into crucifixion plays and Civil War reenactments with David, while I just flung my body around the brown living room shag carpet in Lisa's hand-me-down dance recital tutu, my waist-length hair struggling to keep up with my spasms. Ian also had a developing film guru in his best friend, who pushed him to more refined performance tactics, like charging their younger siblings a nickel just to have the honor of watching their recent play. I, however, was stuck with a quiet, gentle older sister who would rather be playing the piano or flute, and an older brother who'd rather be shoveling manure at our uncle's farm.

"She has fire in her eyes," my aunt Connie said while watching me for the afternoon, only a few months after I'd made it into the world. Her words were embedded in the baby book that I made my mom get down from her closet shelf so frequently growing up. I didn't know what my aunt saw, or how she saw it, in those brand new baby eyes, but over the years as I read those words again and again, I wondered what they would come to mean.

Building on so many years of spunkiness, I felt hopeless to ever be gentle or naturally kindhearted, yet I felt that's exactly what I needed to become in order to help Ian better. Left to my self-analysis, I was too quick to defend myself. I too often forgot to control the tone of my voice and hardly ever held my tongue. If I just had a more tender heart, surely I'd be better for Ian.

"Lord, give me a tender heart," I prayed. "Help me to be more gentle," not knowing that gentleness didn't always need to come in the form of silence.

"That's what he loves about you," Tonya, my college mom, had told me one night on her couch, before the accident, back when my biggest struggle was what to wear on a date. I was already struggling, even then, with this feisty disposition I'd been born with, but Tonya reassured me that Ian loved this trait in me. He hadn't gone looking for a quiet, timid girl.

What I didn't know was that *tender* and *quiet* were about as synonymous as *sultry* and *frigid*. What I didn't yet fully believe was that God had given me this feisty spirit because it was exactly what Ian needed in a wife, the wife that God designed me to be. And with the refining that comes with each day past my birth certificate date, God would use me to help my spouse in the way that He had perfectly created me to be.

My mind was constantly battling these images, rolling over and over in my head, of how women of God are supposed to behave. And if those images were right, then I couldn't possibly say I loved God and be unaccepting of a caregiver at the same time. I couldn't possibly be willing to go to bat against a therapist's perception of Ian's progress and also be gentle. My feistiness felt like it needed to be tamed in order to respond to tragedy well.

Ian wouldn't have agreed. As Tonya said, he wasn't looking for timidity. And his big personality would have trampled it long before the SUV came.

Guilt drifted in that winter, its cold weight pushing beneath my bedroom door. As its fingers stretched up off the floor and into the air of my room, it told me that Ian needed more, deserved more than I could give. It laced its fingers to cup my throat, telling me that Ian needed more therapy, more time in his Bible, more advocacy.

Well, I wasn't interested in spending hours online trying to research new practices or procedures or supplements that could help Ian. I knew there were people like that, but I didn't feel like being one. And yet a new, lingering thought began joining itself to my brain each morning, telling me I needed to fit more into my day so that I could fight harder for Ian.

If these thoughts were meant to motivate me, all they really did was leave me with an ever-present sadness that I would never be enough. There would always be something more I should have done. The game would never be over. The kings on our checkerboard would never all be jumped, conquered, and removed.

I should be more involved with his therapy.

I should be doing more exercises with him at night.

I should be trying for the one hundredth time to find an art therapist or music therapist.

I should be asking the doctors to put him on new medicines or experimental ones or researching all those types of treatments people sent us information for.

All of this guilt billowed up and burrowed in—as it does still—finding and latching onto the places in my heart that are weakest and most susceptible. I would eventually start hearing it even from therapists. Once I became Ian's wife, I'd hear the long lists of what else I needed to be doing for him at home, after I'd worked all day and managed our bills and interacted with caregivers and found time to just be together with Ian each night. And when I'd had all I could stand—dealing with the day and the discouragement from the medical staff who were supposed to be the ones pushing him forward—I often chose the denial route.

I'll do laundry. Normal people do laundry.

One day, already married, and after sobbing for an hour following a meeting with therapists, I decided to lie down on a blanket in the grass instead of going back to work. I threw the laundry into the washer, then later watched it billow and rest, billow and rest, moving with the wind on our backyard clothesline. As I transfixed my eyes onto our pink flowered flat sheet, I became a small girl lying underneath the lines as my mom strung towels and sheets, the summer light revealing my freckles that winter had hidden. A small, trusting girl. Without all the built-up guilt and fear.

But if I held it all up to the light of a God who required nothing more of me than a little girl's mustard seed of faith, I could almost see what happened to guilt when it was slammed against a cross that stood in trio at the top of a hill. And though I couldn't find a Scripture to erase this nagging sense that I couldn't be what Ian needed of me, I did know that I could do all things through Christ. My omissions, my days of choosing rest instead of therapy, even with Ian still in need of repair, would be and already were swept up into Him. I was walking in step with a God who was bigger than me and whose purposes could not be turned awry, and whose enjoyment of me had nothing to do with my works.

And I knew Ian never would—and has never chosen to—point the finger at me and accuse me of anything other than love and hope.

Around Christmas of that year, Ian started using his voice more often. The best time to hear it was while he was sitting on the mat. He wasn't saying words. He wasn't saying our names or telling us what he wanted. But he was creating sounds as he pushed air over his vocal chords and up through his throat.

They were sounds without the tone of his voice, and so they didn't sound familiar. But it was wonderful. We had spent so many hours in speech therapy with a silent Ian, and so many hours sitting by his bed with a silent Ian. And even if all he could get out were moans and grunts, it still meant his mind was starting to remember how to connect to the rest of his body. I would ask him questions I wanted to hear a response to, like "Ian, tell me how much you love me," or "Tell me that I'm your favorite person in the world."

I could decide what his answer sound meant.

And because Ian was starting to use his voice more, I started thinking about marriage more.

I was increasingly encouraged by some of the things Ian was proving able to do—strengthening his leg muscles, moving more intentionally, even being able to replicate a walking motion with the help of a therapist's machine. But I honestly didn't care if I married someone in a wheelchair. That was okay with me. I did, however, need Ian to be able to talk to me. And learning how to use his voice meant that maybe he would soon be forming those groans into words. And maybe the words could grow into a marriage.

I was staying with him because I loved him and because I still believed greater things were yet to come. I was staying with him because I wanted us to be able to make this decision about marriage together, not leave and take it out of his hands.

I had made up my mind I wouldn't leave before he had the chance to tell me what he wanted.

———————

Life on Warren Road was continuing to move forward, from Devon's baseball practice to ballet with Lydia. She posed for a photo in her black leotard and matching tights before we loaded her in the car for her first-ever class. It made me feel special that I was the one to take her. I wanted her to love it. But she wanted to be sitting with me instead of dancing, so we didn't make it past one class.

Caleb was starting to sing in public, meaning out from behind his closed bedroom door. Devon was the first one to hear him singing, which happened by accident. Whether from lack of confidence or just not caring enough, Caleb had never let us hear his voice until it slipped out in front of Devon. After that, we started to see and hear what Caleb had been spending so much time on as he wandered around the house, always with guitar in hand, working on his recent song.

But while we were all just starting to peel back layers that had been protecting us, the lives of our closest friends were moving on. While Ian was trying just to get his left arm to move on command, his next youngest brother and his best friend were dating girls they would soon make their wives.

David was the first of those closest to Ian to move toward marriage. Mary and I stood in the kitchen as David told us about his plan to propose in D.C. He knew, of course, the simmering sorrows this would raise to the brim, and so he wanted us to hear it first from him instead of second- or third-hand.

Mary and I both started crying when he told us. I can't say that I knew the heart cause for Mary's tears, but for me it felt like pure sorrow for Ian blended with jealousy. The comparison of where these best friends lives were headed was so unmatched. Ian would not be able to adequately rejoice with his best friend's gratefulness or give the best man's speech he'd been waiting years to give because he was trapped inside his brain.

Yet we all knew what Ian would have wanted—not guilt, but hope. His love for his friends meant he would not desire to see them suffer or feel anguish over the joys they were coming into, simply because he couldn't know them himself. He would not want others to be held back, even in their minds, because of a traumatic brain injury.

Then two months after David proposed, Ian's brother also proposed to *his* girlfriend . . .

My *best* friend—Jan.

Still wrestling through the darkness of my grief, I didn't know what to do with myself when they told us as we arrived at her parents' house for a birthday dinner. The only thing I knew how to do was congratulate them and then dutifully ask them to take Ian inside for me. I said I'd be inside in a few minutes. But instead I drove away, sobbing.

Sobbing for Ian and the life he had lost and the chances he was unable to take. Sobbing that this couple we loved so much would bring into our home every day the reminder that Ian was sick as they talked about wedding plans and where they would live and the future they would create.

I drove and I parked and I screamed at God for doing this to Ian, and for giving me a grief that could drive a wedge between me and my best friend. Because try as I might, my heart could not fully rejoice with her. It was too weighted down with sorrow. I don't think it would be true to say that I didn't want happiness for them. I did. They had practically become my own siblings. Maybe, in fact, that's exactly why it was so hard. I just didn't yet know what it meant to be long-suffering. Ben and Jan, and David and Sarah, and Marky and Emma, and Adam and Pami were all prospering in the way that I felt most afflicted. All of their lives were moving on. But ours were not. Ian's was not. And it wasn't marriage that I wanted so badly, but simply for the gaps between September 30 and now to not be there.

I thought toward the weddings Ian would be in that summer, starting to miss even more the way it felt to be special to someone, someone who could tell me I was special. Before the accident, Ian had made me his priority in the perfectly small ways, like finding me in a room and coming to sit next to me, or somehow finding a way to get next to me in a crowded car. Those little affections and nods were gone, and all I was left to feel was emptiness, even while he was sitting right next to me. A gap had formed that day in September, and now as it grew, I had to keep looking back to what he used to show me and try to let that hold me. I had to learn how to be the pursuer, whether that meant finding him in a room or planning a date. I was getting scared because I didn't feel the "butterflies" anymore, and I sometimes didn't know what was keeping me in love. I was praying that God would somehow, miraculously, grow a romantic love between us, even when Ian had so few tools at his disposal.

Watching winter melt away into April meant looking at all the new life around us. What was arid was turning green. And how I longed for the turning of nature to materialize inside the walls of Ian's bedroom. I could see and feel God's promises of new life as the warm winds came in behind the cold, yet I was still waking up each morning into a relationship that felt locked away in the barrens. There were things inside of Ian that I felt were still there, and if unlocked would give him a future. Yet unlike the buds outside, all his growth remained locked inside. So the turning of seasons were only pleasant on the surface, because they reminded me of what I was so longing for. They reminded me of what was withheld.

I can't say those losses were not unmet by well-timed graces. The two continued to mingle themselves into a heart that was sorrowful, yet tried to always be rejoicing. "Thus the life of grace is the dawn of immortality," John Newton wrote, "beautiful beyond expression, if compared with the night and thick darkness which formerly covered us; yet faint, indistinct, and unsatisfying, in comparison of the glory which shall be revealed."

And as true as God's promises for new mercies every morning, He gave me reason to keep going. One night, driving home from Jan's house with tears on my cheeks, thinking of all the joys she and Ben would experience in their upcoming marriage, I got home and went into Ian's room, drawing up close to his adjustable hospital bed. And even without his words, he reached his arm out for me and touched my face, my hair, my arm.

He was showing me. I was special to him.

He loved me.

And God was giving Ian reason, too, to keep going.

———————

The first wedding approached quickly that summer. Ian had made the decision to accept Marky's request to be a groomsman. His answer, of course, meant work for his parents—travel and decisions and sacrificial effort—yet their love motivated them to do whatever was necessary. They packed the Hoyer Lift into the van, putting in the middle seat so I had somewhere to sit. David and Sarah, whose wedding would follow in just a few more weeks, were traveling along with us as well. The weekend would be tough on Ian, but being a faithful friend meant taking on the effort, because that type of love was willing to encompass all challenges.

"It's really hard to get past this cabinet," Steve said as he struggled to get Ian's wheelchair through the hotel room kitchen and into the living room. He eventually cleared the width that must have narrowly passed ADA requirements. Then the fire alarm went off, and Steve ran instinctively out the door.

Half laughing and half panicking because our bags weren't even in the room yet, Mary struggled in her ankle-length cotton skirt to get Ian out of the room. "I'll push the leg rests from the front," I said. We struggled and slammed Ian forward and backward, hitting cabinets and living room furniture before eventually being released into the safety of the hallway.

"Umm . . . where's Steve?" I asked.

Realizing at this point that the alarm was purely a drill, we amusedly began looking for Ian's dad, his God-ordained protector who'd bolted at the sound of danger. We found him outside, chatting with a group of guests, completely unaware of the battle we had just waged against and barely won with the hotel countertop. Thus was born a standing joke and memory—of a fight-or-flight reflex gone in the exact opposite direction—that would grow into years of mockery.

"You totally abandoned your family, including your son in a wheelchair!"

"Think of how guilty you would've felt if that had been real!"

Poor Steve, so often the brunt of jokes, but so often so deserving. Like when he and Mary were bringing Ian home from the hospital for the very first time as a baby. As Steve started to place him in the car seat for the first time, he slammed Ian's head against the top of the car door. A member of his self-appointed "Klutz Club," he took his title of president seriously. Before he had children of his own, he sent an infant that he and Mary were babysitting to the doctor, simply by bouncing him up and down on his lap. The child's leg had somehow gotten caught and twisted under Steve's denim-clad thigh, leading to a level of inconsolable crying that required calling the parents home from their attempt at a date. Or the time he fell down the steps at a work site, losing his Bluetooth, or the day that baby Ben, the next after Ian, fell down the steps because the person carrying him (ahem) slipped and lost his footing.

Somehow, three more kids and many tumbles later, they were all fine.

The day after the fire alarm fiasco was the wedding. We sat in the well-groomed yard of the ceremony venue, behind a historic house. Timidity crept into my heart because I didn't know what it would be like to see Ian pushed down the aisle as everyone else walked. I didn't know what it would look like to see Ian from a different vantage point, watching him from the outside, unlike all the times before when I was the one behind or above his wheelchair.

I caught sight of them, David pushing the wheelchair and my boyfriend down the side of the aisle in his tux, not the center where everyone else walked. Hitting me much quicker than I could have anticipated, I cringed with the built-up sorrow of this life of his—a life that used to be so healthy and vibrant, now so terribly broken, head drooping under the heat of the day as he sat beside the two childhood friends he loved.

In a letter to Ian when he was fourteen, Mary had told him what great friends she saw in Marky and David. She said they were the kind of friends she wanted for her son because they were faithful. And the faithfulness she had seen in those nine-year-old boys was now visibly on display, by a friend not embarrassed to ask her son to be in his wedding, a friend not embarrassed by disability.

Ben and Jan were the next to get married, making their way to the altar under a pink sky recently converted from a passing storm. We had watched the storm approaching through the window upstairs with the other bridesmaids, as guests ducked under tents from the light rain. It was an old farmhouse with bright flowery wallpaper in the bedrooms. We were taking photos in the empty room at the top of the stairs. Ian was downstairs with all of his brothers, trying to stay cool and dry. The storm passed in just enough time to start the wedding only a few minutes late, and the sun erased memories of the panic.

I stood next to Jan, and Ian beside Ben. Standing there, in front of the crowd that loved Ben and Jan and joined in their happiness, I couldn't make eye contact with Mary and Steve, not sure what would happen or pass between us if I did. Instead I looked past Jan, Ben, and our pastor, seeing Ian in his wheelchair, his eyes hidden behind the Ray-Bans that the boys wore down the grassy aisle.

He looked so disabled. The sun hit against his lenses and his head drooped again from the heat. I was afraid he would drool as he sat in front of everyone, afraid certain people in the crowd were probably thinking he shouldn't be up there, thinking he didn't realize what was happening enough to be there. But I knew the pain of seeing him with his brothers was better than seeing him as just another person in the crowd. If he wasn't in the hospital, he needed to be up there, right where he was.

Later that night, after the second storm blew through, clenching us underneath the giant tent, we soaked up the rainwater with our shoes on the concrete patio as we danced to the hand-picked playlist. I pushed Ian's wheelchair to the center of the group and sat on his lap. His cousin Sarah grabbed the rubber padding around the push handles of his wheelchair and circled us around. I laughed as Frank Sinatra swooned and Ian smiled.

He couldn't dance himself, so we made his chair dance.

He was happy.

His joy diverted me to hope.

―――――――

Ian was getting stronger throughout the summer and didn't need the help of the Hoyer Lift anymore. Steve had taken the courageous step of trying a transfer without the lift . . . and it worked. Still, Ian's body didn't move as smoothly as it used to, making any kind of action awkward. But by not being totally dependent on the lift, we didn't need to lug out the clunky metal frame and sling every time we wanted to get him on the couch or in a patio chair. It also meant, instead of perching myself on the thin armrest of his wheelchair, I could sit next to him on a couch or squeeze myself onto the wingback. I didn't need to be across the room from him, where life without his words felt like being in a separate place.

He was eating more food by mouth now, after we chopped it into small pieces—real food like spaghetti and meatballs and eggs. He was also drooling less, now that his mouth and lips were strong enough to close on their own and sense the tickle of wandering saliva. I had grown accustomed to seeing him with a large swatch of wet shirt on his chest from the drool that dripped down. In fact, I rarely noticed it until he began to do it less.

On July 20, we took him to a new therapy office, and were sitting in the waiting room, preparing for his appointment with the swimming pool. But when the therapist arrived, she asked if anyone had ever gotten Ian out of his wheelchair to walk. We watched in terror as she pulled him out of his chair, using her husband as counterbalancing leverage to support Ian's weight. We hadn't seen him standing upright since his accident, not without the Hoyer Lift or the standing machine. I didn't know if I could watch. I was so scared.

But . . . Ian did fine. His therapist proved to us that he could do more than we thought, more than we'd been asking of him.

So again, we headed back to the lake in August for the family vacation. And this time, we had plans to get Ian into the water.

No matter what happened in the months between, the lake didn't age. Time didn't seem to pass, and cousins didn't grow too far apart. Those two weeks at the lake were two weeks that Ian longed for. And since this was my third family vacation here, my own comfort had also begun to settle.

I spent my time either inside the house with Ian or lying on the dock with his cousins. But the highlight of our whole time there was the initiation of our plan to get Ian into the water.

We enlisted all the men in the family to help and found a place on the house property where they could roll his wheelchair somewhat close to the water. From there, they lifted him into a plastic patio chair and carried it into the shallowness of the lake edge. Once they were deep enough, his dad pulled him up out of the chair and into his arms, the buoyancy of the life jacket bobbing him. It was mid-afternoon and the sun was warm, so Ian's uncle offered him his fishing hat.

And there he was. My boyfriend. The one who used to tan in short shorts and aviators on the top deck with his cousins Sarah and Jessie, floating in the water, supported by his dad, in an adult-sized life jacket and a floppy fishing hat.

Ian spent two weeks in November with a cold. Something had moved into his lungs, taking up residence there and making him cough frequently. But I loved his cough . . . because his voice was hidden inside it. That voice needed to be there, in his bedroom and in the van as he rode to a breakfast date. That voice was missing at family dinner or when people stared at him in the store.

I desperately wanted him to be using that voice again. When I said I wanted God to show up in Ian's life, I mainly meant in his throat and in his lungs—to let his words come back to us.

"I get myself in trouble a lot,' Ian had said to me while we were newly dating. "When you talk this much, the chances of saying something dumb are pretty high."

True. I had seen him walk himself into moments of regret quite often and found a lot of joy in witnessing the attempted maneuvers to back out.

What I wouldn't give now to hear another.

And on November 29, I did.

A new, raspy voice pushed out of Ian's throat and into the air of his bedroom. Shrieking, I begged him to make it again, to make sure I wasn't imagining, and to make sure he had said what he meant to say. I had pictured this moment in my head so many times and had forced my memory to try creating the sound. But this time it wasn't just whispering inside my own head. This time it was unmistakable.

"Eee un."

He said . . . Ian.

All of the folders in his brain that were scattered and disarrayed finally gave in to the new cells that were forging, begging to pull together enough just to utter one word. Trapped inside himself for two years, he had fought his way out, against the jumbled letters and words and memories. Like his triplet cousins breaking through the surface of the lake each time they popped back up after a cannonball off the dock, he had kicked back to the top, and had chosen to break through at a moment when I alone was there, giving me this first glimpse into a future that would be able to include his voice. A future that meant when the airbag slammed against his throat and face, it didn't kill what he really needed.

My world was suddenly opening as quickly as Ian's, thinking about all this one word meant. That first word started a new journey through life that had been darkened for so long, phosphorous struck to build light.

———————

I was sitting on the bed, thinking and watching my husband rest, thinking about what life was like when he was in his coma.

"It took my life away for those years," he said. "It's frightening because I don't even know what happened in that time. But I do know one thing that God was doing with my wifey. He was making her a good helper. He was preparing me for living life again."

nine

run away from it, my heart tugging at my legs to run and run faster—away from the darkness, away from the unknown, through the huge bushes of burdock, running toward something that looks brighter and less fearsome.

Finally a house comes into view, its bay window and pink azalea bushes inviting me toward it. Slowing a little, I walk swiftly through the grass that someone has loved enough to manicure and look up at the dormers just below the roof. The siding is light gray, and the windows that line up together across the front porch form almost a smile.

He sits there on the swing chained to the roof ceiling, looking at me with his lips curled into a grin. He waves, holding a glass of lemon water in his left hand. When returned to his lap, his hands lie comfortably together as he cups the glass and his toes gently push the swing back and forth, back and forth. A breeze tickles his brown bangs and sideburns, and a single red lantern swings to his rhythm on the edge of the porch.

Climbing the steps, drawing closer, I look down at the hardwood porch floor covered with a delicate hook rug, colors faded with happy wear. I see a pacifier and follow the trail of hints to a toddler girl, her back to me as she stacks blocks to show her daddy.

Something tells me this is *my* house, that it's *my* little girl, *my* groom. And yet I seem to know that I have no business being here, that I'm mistaken to be running this way. The home and the comfort and the stillness are pulling me, but I know I must go back, must turn into the darkness and follow it.

Before going, though, I need to open the door first.

He looks at me and the toddler looks at me. My shaky hand clasps the door handle, turning and hoping. The door slips open and as the hinges shift, I feel the tumble of a beam, and notice my shoulder is covered in the white flakes of loosened drywall. I look up at the doorframe and the ceiling above it as they start to cave from the inside out. The house begins to crumble, as if there's no foundation, as if it had been built of tissues or cardboard or expectations or naïveté.

My groom scoops up my toddler from her blocks and sweeps past me, into the falling frame, covering themselves under the dust and imploded roof. *Why have they gone running into this? And why without me?*

Soon, it is all dust. Fallen with just a touch.

I turn slowly to look behind me at the dark trail I'd come from. The disintegrated house lies in waste, a house that wasn't meant to stand. I beg for the light of the home to come back, for his grin to come back, for this scene to reconstruct itself out of the rubble. I'm not ready to keep walking into the blackness, and yet the house had fallen too easily. The home I had seen was built too quickly, too hurriedly. There must have been something in the darkness

I hadn't seen yet, something I flew by in my haste to reach this brighter place.

Slowly, I reach for the red lantern, still lit even after the tumult. I clasp the handle and step closer toward the blackness. Turning around, my memory etches the outline of the house before it fell and locked him and her away. I step backward onto the thick gravel of the darker road, walking so that the invisible house is always in my view. As the darkness grows deeper around me, its thickness makes the open sores in my heart leak out. And as the sores leak, the darkness melds into me, ballooning up where those sores had been, filling me. The darkness makes me move more slowly, and the deeper it becomes, the scarier my image of the destroyed house looks.

I can't look any longer. I must turn into this darkness—a darkness becoming so dense that I must push against it with my arms out in front of me, pushing it forward with every step. The thickness of the air holds me upright. The red lantern in my hand sees my bare toes peeking out beneath me. But the further I walk, the more its light expands, until it opens up wider and fuller and more vibrant, displacing the molecules that made up the dense fog . . . and I know why I am there.

The light has broken into the darkness.

The darkness could not withstand the light.

———————

At the start of 2009, we reflected back on our blog to the past year and all that God had accomplished. It was the year that Ian ate food for the first time. The year that he talked for the first time. Each day, God was giving a little bit of Ian back to us. Piece by piece, He was re-building Ian, even though the blocks He was using were different than they'd been in Mary's womb.

I asked God for 2009 to be a year filled with more laughter than tears, more prosperity than sorrow. I asked that it be the year that Ian be delivered. I was growing weary of learning about God through deep waters and wanted instead to come to know Him in gentleness and prosperity.

The progress that Ian was making wasn't changing my grief. With two years under my belt, I was learning that the only thing time did to grief was make it more dull. It wasn't the same intensity as when we were in the hospital but instead it was taking root and permanence. I was learning that this grief, the grief of a brain injury, wasn't going to end. I was starting to see that I would forever on earth be grieving a death of Ian as I sat and cheered him on in therapy. Even as Ian would come to know Christ more, he would also come to know loss more, every day, every day that he woke up with legs and arms and a brain that didn't work like he wanted.

Every once in awhile Ian's voice would come out as he struggled to talk again, but mostly he was only mouthing words to us. I was working on becoming a lip reader, and he was working on understanding the importance of breath and coordinating his vocal chords to his teeth and tongue. He was growing frustrated and obviously angry that he couldn't figure it all out. Yet he didn't give up.

For my twenty-fourth birthday, Ian's family helped him plan a date that included dinner and driving back to find the dining room set up with chocolate cake for two. More than the food, however, Ian gave me the best gift of all that night when he laughed—a laugh so hard and so authentic that it almost sounded like the old Ian. It was the happiest he'd sounded in two and a half years. The pictures from that night looked better too, because they looked like he was really there. Most photos from past days revealed empty eyes, eyes you might expect from someone with a brain injury. In these photos, though, they looked full.

He was here.

And he was still in love with me.

And seeing that Ian was starting to "be here" made me start thinking that marriage might really be an option.

I had been praying that God would divert my affection for Ian if our life wasn't going to lead to marriage. Steve had encouraged me one day in the kitchen that God could grant us the desires of our hearts if they were desires rooted in a longing for holiness and not sin. And as I prayed, and as we lived, I could tell my affection for Ian wasn't ending, but was only growing deeper and more intense, even after spending more than two years sitting by his bed hoping to hear words.

> *March 15, 2009*
> Ian, most of my smiles in one day come from you. I smile looking at you and even thinking of you. I am amazed and constantly encouraged by your battle—you have run this race with endurance and perseverance. You continue to work so diligently to come back to us (and me specifically). I am so blessed to know you and get to experience this love. It is so truly God that allows us to not only love but enjoy each other. We are so limited physically and our conversations are way too much one-sided. Our situation would so quickly grow stagnant with our relationship because of our limitations. But God is kind in that it seems like He refreshes us each day. I love you. Come back.

One night in May, before I said good night to Ian, I asked him what he wanted prayer for. Because his speech was getting better, he was able to start asking for prayer in certain areas of his life. But after giving his answer that night, he asked me how he could pray for me.

I was stunned.

I was caught off guard.

It was exactly what we had been praying for—for him to be able to initiate.

Having him able to tell us he was hungry—that was great, a vast improvement, a reason to celebrate his progression. But knowing better how to care for his soul was a priceless joy, a miracle.

I had been praying for him for what felt like forever, not really knowing how to pray, and not knowing at all if he was praying for me in return. He couldn't give me the evidence by doing it out loud. But the more that Ian was talking, the clearer it was becoming to us that his soul was fine. Somewhere inside that cloud of coma, he was fine.

———————

Ian became an uncle on June 19, 2009. He was instantly in love and ready to hold and snuggle on his new nephew. Ian met Paladin just a few hours after he arrived into our lives, his perfectly made body wrapped into a blankie. Ian was happy, his lips quickly marching into the position of a genuine smile, a practiced formation that was showing up more often the further Ian got away from 2006.

A few months prior, while we were still anticipating this new entrant into our lives, someone asked Ian how he felt about soon becoming an uncle.

"Avuncular," he said.

He said it a few more times before we correctly interpreted.

Avuncular?

We grabbed a dictionary because we thought we knew what it meant, but his vocabulary was obviously better than ours.

"Of or like an uncle," Mary read from the thick dictionary, the one that had provided so many similar insights during the Murphys' homeschooling days. And our "avuncular" Ian didn't stop smiling the whole time he held all six pounds of his new favorite person.

I was so happy for him, and so hopeful that someday, if we ever had a baby, he could hold that new life—maybe with the help of a supporting hand, but yet still holding him. Here was a new person for Ian to love, and a new person to find joy in him. We didn't know then that Paladin and all of our future nieces and nephews would show Ian the purest type of love. We didn't know that with each year of Paladin's life, we would more and more hear ourselves saying, "He's exactly like Ian." In the meantime, he brought everyone in the hospital room the excitement of hope that life could start new.

We visited Paladin again later that afternoon. Mary and I were on our way to a wedding, an outdoor affair on a calm June afternoon. Jan lamented that she would have to miss it, her body well-worn from the labor twelve hours before. So as Mary and I drove the back roads to the grassy field wedding, I kept thinking about how I wasn't as sad going to this wedding as the ones the summer before. Maybe it was a baby hangover. Or the transparent sky above the roof of Mary's blue Taurus.

Or maybe just God.

We sat down on the bride's side a few rows from the rear. Gigi found us, and soon enough we were laughing. I watched the bridesmaids walk from what would be the couple's new home together, and then watched as the tea-length clothed bride made her way to the front.

For the first time since Ian's accident, the weight of watching two people excitedly stand before a pastor didn't bow my head into tears. For the first time in a long time, I wasn't sad. I felt happy and I felt hopeful. I felt as if I wasn't alone.

Marriage felt closer.

"Ian, what's the first thing you'd do if God totally healed you?" I asked him in my tankini one bright afternoon as we sat beside our pastor's pool. I was trying to take Lydia to the pool often so she could enjoy her summer and so I could have an excuse to lie in the hot sun with my skin against the rough concrete. Ian was in his wheelchair, which kept him a few feet above the pool edge. I was thinking about all the ways I would answer that question if I were asked, and I could see in my mind, things like . . . jumping in the pool, sweeping Lydia and I into a dance, running to his mom's house.

Ian, however, while I was thinking of these "doings," was on a different surface.

"Thank Him."

As often as we could, we traveled with Caleb to hear gigs he'd scheduled around and near Pittsburgh. I labeled Ian and I as his biggest fans, going to the outreach center where he played in front of ten senior citizens, driving for two hours to play in a coffee shop with two guests other than us (who happened to be friends from Pittsburgh meeting us there).

The life of a young artist, I guess, is hard. But the gigs gave us something to do and gave us a way to show Caleb that Ian could still be in his life.

After one particular show we sat in the car while Caleb ran inside a store to use the restroom. I got bored and started filming Ian, asking him what he thought Caleb was doing in the store and why it was taking him so long. It was the longest amount of talking that Ian had done, and I caught it all on camera as he cut jokes and repeated himself seventeen times until I could understand it.

Luck? No.

Stuck? No.

Tongues? No.

Dungs? No.

Turns out the word was "dunked." He laughed at me the whole time as I guessed, and the sequence of words often enters conversations now with his brothers because my interpretations were so off.

"Ian, what would you do if someone broke into our van? How would you protect me?"

[Pause.]

"Point at the sign."

"What sign?"

"Giant Eagle," he said, the name of the store Caleb was inside.

"What would that do?"

"I'd ask them how to spell it."

I burst out laughing.

"As a means of distraction?"

"Yeah."

"And what would *you* do when they looked at the sign?"

"I'd run."

"What about me?"

"I'd tell you to come."

I wanted to marry Ian. Yet I also wanted to keep waiting, because stalling out of fear was more comfortable than jumping in with faith. I didn't really know what it would mean to marry someone in Ian's health. He loved my soul, but I didn't know if love for my soul could fill the gaps I would feel in my heart.

So we just kept going. And so did I.

And so did Ian.

We prepared to head to the lake again in August, looking forward to nights of setting suns reflecting on the water and rests in the shade with Paladin, our toes dipping into the lake. Mary, Lydia, and Ian loaded up the van and drove south while Steve and I stayed behind in town a day or two for work. The morning Steve left to drive himself to the lake, he was supposed to leave a house key out for me. I'd been staying with Ben and Jan and would be driving over to the Murphys the next day to finish packing my bags before heading out. But when I got there, I couldn't find the key. I looked in all the normal hiding places and went around to the lower entrance to Ian's addition, but everything was locked. I finally got in touch with Steve by cell phone and asked him where the key was.

"It's inside on the kitchen table."

"Steve, do you realize that I can't get to the kitchen table because the door is locked?"

Pause. Then realization.

Not typical of Steve. He clearly hadn't thought that one through.

Fortunately for me, there were a few windows at ground height that were unlocked, so I made my way through one of them, projecting out onto the hardwood floor on the other side.

I had first met Steve at a campfire the Murphys hosted for college students. Then after Ian and I were dating, our first interaction was at church. "We're really excited to see what happens," he had said to me in a group of people. It was awkward, because it implied he was expecting something more from me than just dating his son for a few weeks and then breaking up. I was expecting more too, but it was awkward to hear my boyfriend's dad say it out loud.

His awkwardness, I soon found out, was more than par for the course, and it was soon endearing to me. I didn't have many memories of him before the accident, except for family dinners where he did most of the listening. After everything happened that day on Route 422, however, I learned to know Steve very differently, in the way his family had always known him. Ian had always taken his questions to his dad to seek his counsel. He knew there was a dear and godly friend to be found in his dad, as long as Ian humbled himself in honor to him.

Steve knew that what was happening to Ian inside of his coma was hurting me, and he took an interest in caring for my soul while I lived under his roof. Not afraid of hard conversations, he would ask me questions that quickened my heart to Jesus. During days of commuting around to work sites, stopping into the hospital for a visit with Ian, and then taking care of his wife and four kids at home, he still found time to answer those questions of mine that brought me so much confusion.

"Why do we keep praying for Ian to be healed?"

"Did God give this brain injury, or just allow it? And either way, why?"

"How do I have joy in this?"

Some questions really haunted me. And before Ian could talk, Steve was his voice for him, helping to shepherd me through the words that God had already laid out for me and for many saints before me. He was standing in front of his family, walking in front of his family, gently showing us how to continue in truth among the thorny vines and smoke-clogged streets. He poured truth into his family, large vessels tipping over and streaming forth fruit as we watched how he walked, how he led, how he regarded his Savior. He always regarded the Lord delicately, timidly, for he knew the path had already been laid out for him, as well as for his oldest son. He just laid back and let mercy carry him.

Simply, he was a good man who loved his family.

After breaking into the house to find the key that Steve had left on the table, I made my way to the lake in my new 4Runner, listening to the latest Coldplay album that later marked the end of that summer in my memory. I joined the cousins and Ian in sitting by the water and floating on the black inner tubes that Grandpa brought. We rode on the flotilla, Uncle Eric's boat pulling two ropes, each flanked with swimmers on tubes, hands gripped onto the rope as he drove us around the lake. We celebrated Aunt Andrea's cooking at the annual luau and cooled off inside to *Alfred Hitchcock Presents* and late-night hours of home improvement shows. Ian still had to be careful how much time he spent outside during the warmest parts of the day, and Steve had a head cold, so those two Murphy men spent a lot of time inside.

We came home on Saturday, August 16, to our fractured normalcy, settling Ian back into his comfortable bedroom and roll-in shower. I went back to work on Monday morning.

Normal.

Then—on Wednesday, August 20—our new normal collided again with nightmare.

"Mama, Daddy fell out of bed," Lydia told Mary. She had been lying next to him, watching Winnie the Pooh, then had run downstairs to find Mary as soon as Steve's body hit the floor. Mary knew this wasn't something Steve would do to entertain their four-year-old daughter, so she ran quickly up the stairs to find her husband of twenty-seven years convulsing on their bedroom floor.

Caleb was home and had learned about seizures in college. He knew the most dangerous part was the probability that Steve would swallow his tongue. So he held his father down and rolled him to his side. He felt the pulsing and thuds of his dad's body as it jerked around the hardwood floor. Lydia found Ian and I downstairs, and I held her as we prayed against . . . what? We didn't know.

Later that night we found ourselves in the same ER waiting room, the same one where the caseworker had met us with Ian's wallet three years earlier. All of the siblings were there again, except for little Lydia. Some of the Altrogges were there too, David's family. We were led upstairs to the same wing of the hospital where a new doctor told us that Steve had a tumor on his brain, and that it had grown to the size of a grapefruit. So we found ourselves nodding numbly in agreement when we were told emergency surgery was needed, and that we would need to wait until after the surgery to find out if it was cancerous or benign.

The Murphys and the Altrogges, all sitting together, distracting ourselves from hearing the surgery results. I left to call Mary's niece Jessie, to say that her uncle was in emergency brain surgery, and could she please tell the rest of the family?

Back in the waiting room, someone wanted us to pray together as a group, and as I sat next to Ian in his power wheelchair, holding his left hand and hoping he was piecing this all together, someone started to pray.

They were the same prayers.

The same Scripture.

The same hospital wing on Lothrop Street, Pittsburgh— hearing the same words that had been prayed for Ian.

The memories ballooned inside my chest, still growing as I escaped through the door and sank to the floor under the support of the nearest bathroom wall behind me, begging God to undo all that had been done. The smell and the people and the prayers seemed like they had never left Unit 4G, because they all looked and sounded and smelled the same as when they had been prayed for Ian, trapped inside ICU walls where those kind of prayers are needed the most.

My eyes dripped with new tears, falling on my cheeks, as I struggled to believe that our lives were in the ICU again. We needed Steve, but he wasn't there.

"I don't believe it's God's will for Steve to die," someone told me downstairs a few minutes later, near the bathrooms at the bottom of the escalator where we walked when we needed a breath.

"I'm glad that you feel that," I said. "But it's not guaranteed to us, and we need to prepare in case Steve dies."

Belief is harder earned when it's your life in the hospital bed.

It was the same plight we found ourselves in again, preparing for our lives to change.

We found out later that night, as the gentle surgeon sat with us, that the grapefruit ballooning inside of his brain was indeed cancerous. Treatable, but not curable. The words entered my ear canals and tumbled around inside my brain as I tried to absorb the letters fused together into a death sentence.

Nine of us spent the next four days crammed into a hospital room with a two-month-old Paladin and tried to celebrate Devon's birthday on August 22. I picked up cake and gifts that were supposed to be from Mary and Steve. We tried to act like serving cake on hospital paper towels and getting interrupted to hook your dad up to an EEG were normal birthday activities. Steve was talking and kept reminding us that God knew, knew exactly what He was doing, no matter how sad we were.

He came home to a schedule of chemotherapy and radiation and therapy. Just like Ian, he lost strength in his arm and found himself being asked to do therapies he had previously done with his son.

Then on September 1, this new reality came with a name. And a number.

Steve was formally diagnosed with a type of brain cancer. He told us on the patio that night, as he pulled up a stool and carefully sat himself and his tears down. I looked around at his four sons sitting underneath the weight of the afternoon sun and wondered what those words felt like for Steve.

What those words felt like for Steve . . .

"They said I have fourteen weeks to live."

I wondered what happened inside, what had to bubble up to form and utter eight words that meant his sons were about to lose their dad. I wondered what he felt when he saw Ian half-slumped into the sun's heat and knew his son was losing his best advocate. I wonder what he saw when he looked at heaven so near.

September 2, 2009 (Steve)

Cancer is not in the Bible, but death is. We have ways of forestalling death, even death from cancer. They had the ability to forestall my death a little longer, and I'm amazed that I'm still alive. But some day my death is going to come. I'm so grateful the Bible teaches me what God did to save me from death. I'm so grateful that I don't have to be deserving in order to gain Christ.

This news meant we would all spend the next few weeks helping Ian remember what was happening, because his short-term memory was so weak. I tried to remind him of the cancer and of the fourteen weeks and of the treatable but not curable diagnosis. I tried to talk to him about all of the things he loved about his dad and tried to pray together as a family for healing and for strength if heaven came.

For me, and for Ian, so many of our conversations with Steve over the last few weeks of Steve's life were about our future together. Steve wanted us to make a decision, either to separate or marry, but he didn't want to watch us stay in the limbo of dating. Steve talked to Ian a lot, like the time I found them out on the patio, and Steve started to tell me what he was learning in the book of Job, and what Ian had been telling him about wanting to marry me.

Steve was helping Ian to prepare to make one of the biggest decisions of his life.

Later that night I was in the dining room, ironing, while Ian was in the shower. The air in the house felt cool and fresh, moving in through the windows from the fall outside. Steve came into the room and sat down at the table, and I told him I felt different. I could only explain it like Aslan from the Narnia stories, how it felt like God was on the move. It felt like we were on the verge of something with Ian, maybe a healing. It felt like Ian was coming back to me.

And I hated to think about his dad not being there to see it.

"Ian!" I exclaimed, "I think we could leave the house tonight without your wheelchair!"

"Okay."

I put the brace on my husband's bad leg, the New Balance sneaker with a rubber wedge melded to the bottom to compensate for the difference in height from a knee that doesn't straighten. He stands and I strap his arms into his walker with the armrest attachments . . . because his arms don't straighten either.

He starts taking steps out of our bedroom and onto the patio. A light breeze pushes him along in his walker as he steps away from the house without a wheelchair for the first time in seven years. He spends fifteen minutes walking a path to the car that normally takes me thirty seconds, but he's doing it. And it's a gift.

"How does this feel, Ian, to leave the house without your wheelchair," I ask once we make it to the car and his tired legs can rest.

"It feels freeing."

He's still accomplishing, still gaining, and God is still working in him. We can't accept the "nots," the assumption that Ian is unable to do things. Because nothing is ever accomplished by not trying.

"Caleb, do you think we could get Ian in the golf cart?"

We do—two and a half years after we unsuccessfully tried the same at our wedding.

"Ian, I feel like you could drive the golf cart."

"This is a bad idea," he says, after his left foot has found the gas and his left hand the wheel. Bad idea, maybe, but it turns into a fruition that makes me squeal so loudly with delight, our aunt can hear us across the field. Fortunately the edges of the lake are far and the grass of the sports fields are wide, perfect for a man who's spent seven years under the control of others.

"Do you think we could get Ian on the four-wheeler?"

"Do you think we could stand here next to each other, just holding hands instead of your arm being around me? I've always been jealous of photos that other couples have, just standing next to each other, and I want her to take a picture of us like that today."

"Ben, do you think we could get Ian on the hot air balloon ride here?"

"Do you think we could walk up the steps of this house instead of never coming over to visit?"

We can't accept the assumptions, because we're starting to see there's a life to live outside of the comfortable walls of our suite and the comfortable padding of a wheelchair. As he does sit-ups each night and strengthens himself with the help of his caregiver, we decide to use those muscles to accomplish joys for him, like the freedom of driving himself around in a golf cart, hoping that one day he can golf again, a sport he enjoyed so much. We can't keep accepting the limitations, because one day the not trying will lead to not able.

We can't accept the limitations because, as far as we know, God has not put them on us or on Ian's body.

"The LORD will fulfill his purpose for me" (Ps. 138:8).

———

A few days later, exactly four weeks after Steve's seizure, I was sitting at the kitchen table eating breakfast. I heard something strange come from Ian's bedroom, and I heard his caregiver making unusual expressions and sounds.

Something sounded like groaning. Or sputtering. Mary went in because she heard it too, and then she came out looking for the phone.

"What's wrong?" I asked as she started to dial 9-1-1.

I didn't get an answer right away, because they wanted to protect me, but I knew something was wrong. I kept asking. I kept asking to go in.

When I did, I found Ian in the middle of a seizure, his body convulsing and his eyes blank.

"Ian, look at me!" I begged. I tried to hold him, tried to get him to focus. I was so scared that everything had been lost.

The ambulance came, and as they were strapping Ian onto the gurney, I met Steve stepping out of the den. Seeing him made the tears comfortable enough to make their way out of my eyes, and they fell onto his shoulder.

"I can't do this again," I said.

"Do what?" he asked gently.

"This."

What I meant but couldn't build into sentences was another hospital for Ian and another seizure for a man in my life.

We all made our way to the local hospital again, as I rode in the ambulance alongside Ian. We waited on the cushioned chairs and stared at the daytime programming on the wall TVs and hoped this wasn't a brain tumor. Ben called my mom because I didn't have words. The pastors came, and I tried to talk from within my inside-out university hoodie and Ian's old sweatpants. Steve came, but Caleb had to take him across the street for his radiation treatment before we knew if Ian was okay.

Once we were allowed inside, I sat next to Ian's bed and held his left hand, just as I had done in the ICU. Gigi came into the room, too, because just like the heart monitor, she was a fixture in hospital rooms with us now. She had her coffee and a free hand to rub my back. Then I walked alongside Ian's gurney to the MRI.

And then, relief.

The results came back normal. Yes, the doctor said, it was odd, to have an onset of seizures so late after the initial injury, but it was actually sort of a good thing—good because the seizures indicated regrowth as the neurons fought against damaged brain tissue to forge new pathways.

We returned home, still on our journey of precariously balancing hope and reality. Laughter just had to be a part of our survival—the therapy sessions, the family dinners laced with sadness. Otherwise the impending moments of growing brain tumors became simply too much. We needed the relief, the outlook, and the benefit of vibrating diaphragms.

We needed each other.

And we didn't know how much more time we'd have.

We were seeing more of each other, all of us, as a family. Ben, who had recently graduated from college, was offered a job three hundred miles away but knew that he and Jan and Paladin, and their future children, needed to be closer, needed to be nearby to be with his mom. It was a decision that unknowingly meant several more years of job hunting, watching God provide in unexpected ways, including two more babies and a house they never would have dreamed of affording.

Caleb, a few years and a wedding day later, had moved to California with his new wife for the warm, dry air—a welcome relief for her chronic migraines—only to realize they also needed to be with their families. It meant giving up a chance for his wife to have health and relief, but they knew it would be empty relief if family weren't there.

Five days after Ian's ER visit, Steve found himself there as well, the seizures taking over his body again. He was life-flighted again because the tumor was growing again. He had been having a harder time talking, an unknown indicator of tumor growth. We now had before us a decision, just like when we sat in the stark family room three years before, trying to weigh the value of life support for Ian. We had a choice to go ahead with a surgery that carried a significant chance of further deteriorating Steve's speech and other abilities, or we could do nothing and hope the tumor didn't spread too quickly.

As we stood around the hospital bed and monitors, I recalled the conversation on the patio, the conversation where Steve encouraged me that whatever we decided about marriage, someday we would need to look back and know that we had made the decision in faith. That's what we had to do here also, in that room as Paladin lay sleeping in Jan's arms and Lydia stood by the foot of the bed that her daddy never wanted her to see.

So we made the decision to have the second surgery. And Steve came home a few days later.

From there he continued to deteriorate.

As he was getting weaker, it was harder for him to come downstairs, eventually impossible. And since Ian couldn't go upstairs, he didn't get to spend much time with his dad as he slipped into death.

Finally we realized that Steve wasn't going to come down again, which meant we needed to do whatever it took to get Ian up. Three brothers and his best friend struggled to carry him up the steps, and place him into his dad's office chair that we pushed to the side of the bed where Steve slept. Steve was still keeping his eyes open, but he wasn't talking.

There they sat. And lay.

In the saddest of silence.

I tried to see Steve when I could, checking in with Mary throughout the day to see if I could just go sit with him and talk to him. One afternoon I found the perfect time, just after I'd met with our pastor about marrying Ian. "Do you feel pressured to stay?" our pastor had asked me. Had the expectations of our families, or the story we'd tried to capture on the blog, or the weakness of my own heart come together to corner me into a trap? No, I didn't think so. I truly thought Ian and I could marry.

"I promise you we'll take care of Ian," I told Steve's thinning body that day, looking into his face that was growing so hollow and slight. "I promise you I'll take care of him."

He was leaving behind his adult disabled son. We had to promise him.

Steve's mind continued to slip away. One afternoon he spent fifteen minutes pointing to the screen on his phone, trying to get it to do something, trying to tell me something. It wasn't a touch-screen phone, so he wasn't able to get it to do whatever he wanted. He just looked at me, begging me to unleash what was being trapped in his brain, what was being trapped by the words he could no longer utter.

Because the cancer was winning.

My husband is working so hard to get stronger. I look at him standing to my right, his arms strapped onto the walker and the brace keeping his right knee stable. He's been working on walking, even these six years after the accident. His therapist wants him to stand for an hour each night. And tonight he picked to walk to the living room. So now he stands by me, in front of the couch.

"Ian, maybe if you sing, it will help the time to pass," I say to him as I watch the timer I've set on my phone.

"That sounds like a selfish request."

"Because I love to hear you sing?"

He laughed his reply "yes."

His legs start to shake as they grow tired, and he tries to squat and sit down. Feeling like a nag but trying to do what the therapist says, I tell him he can't sit yet. Caleb holds the walker so that Ian doesn't lose balance and topple over . . . again.

As I'm sitting here, able to position my body in whatever way I want, I look at him and wonder what it's like to be inside *his* body. I wonder what it's like to need a piece of equipment just to be able to stand. I wonder how he faces each session of standing without growing weary.

"Ian, what keeps you working hard?"

"You."

"Why?"

"Because you're a reward."

"How?

"Hugs and kisses."

Caleb and I laugh at his answer as I tuck myself under my husband's left arm. Caleb sits across from us reading on the pink Victorian couch disguised white by the yard sale slipcover. Caleb's laugh, a regular fixture to our nights at home, gives away his thoughts.

"Mocking." Ian calls him out.

I know I need to store this moment in my heart because the enjoyment, the interactions, won't always be there. Coming ahead and having passed are likely days when Ian won't be able to express his appreciation for me, maybe because he's too tired or maybe because he has another bladder infection that's robbing him of his only faculties. This moment needs to be tucked into my heart so that when sly doubt creeps into the silences in our bedroom, I can look back and remind myself of all the times when he showed me his tenderness, when he showed me that he loved me.

Those were the costs that Ian had to consider before choosing to propose. Those were the questions he had to process through and throw against Scripture to see how they landed.

Will God take care of my wife?

Will I be able to keep loving her?

Can my disabled body make a good husband?

God needs to be tucked in there too, though, filling bigger spaces and plugging emptier holes, because the bad brain injury days feel unbearable—or even just the ones when I can't see past his lacks, when the days start to feel like eternity.

"Ian, I can't do this," I sometimes say on those days.

"I don't want this."

"I'm suffocating from this."

Drowning in thoughts of the things he can't do can sometimes launch an angry voice from my lungs, far too often for a wife. It means more reminders to stop holding his right hand because it's starting to deform the muscles, more begging him to please keep his head down, more "Ian, I have no idea what you're saying. You have to speak more clearly."

It means hormones—the most unfortunate suffocation of all, a most vulnerable time for my heart as chemistry mixes into reality and makes a brain-injured cacophony.

I know that I can't listen to those thoughts, can't act on them or try to validate them. Instead I need to push them back with the force of knees bent.

Truth must win. It *has* to win.

Christ is Lord over death. Over suffering. Over all.
It is why we keep on battling.

———————

"I think today is the day, Gigi."

My fingers somehow texted the words to Gigi, just after
I cancelled our plans to walk on the Hoodlebug, a small
walking trail through our town. Somehow it felt like it was
the day, the morning that Steve was going to die.

Sitting in the living room, I watched Mary's brief appear-
ances downstairs, watched her demeanor, and recalled the
two nights before when I'd asked how much longer. I was
upset because I wasn't being told, but we knew it wasn't
good. I knew it wasn't good because I'd walked in on Mary
talking with a new nurse . . . a hospice nurse.

"Well, he's not drinking anymore, and he can only live a
few days without liquids."

Mary came in the living room after I texted Gigi.

"Caleb?" Mary said—Mary had quietly walked downstairs from her room—"I think he's close to the end. Come
up now if you want to say good-bye to your dad." I didn't
move from my chair because I wasn't their daughter. I was
there only because of a son who'd just left with his caregiver
for therapy. Somehow, though, in the tense moments that
followed, I ended up in the doorway of their room, two of
her sons and her young daughter sitting on the bed edges.

Steve's body was there, but that was all.

I left to tell Ian, making my way to the hospital. I whispered to his therapist, then drove Ian's chair out of the
speech room where he had worked so hard for too many
days. I told him in a hospital parking lot that his dad was
gone. Jan came and met us outside after leaving her shift on

the seventh floor telemetry unit. We reminded Ian again. Then we all drove off so Jan could find Ben at the school where he was substitute teaching, and tell him too.

Back to the living room, back to the sight of our nurse friend flushing OxyContin down the toilet, counting each pill to make sure we didn't keep any for ourselves, we saw the funeral home workers come—strangers to us—wrap Steve's body into a bag, and carry him past us, down the one set of split-entry steps. I turned my back to them because I didn't want to know what bodies look like when they're wrapped tight in bags.

We were back in time for the stillness to come.

We were back in time to sit there in the living room: Mary, her four sons, a daughter-in-law, her little girl, and her new grandbaby. And me. We were back in time to sit and start to process, and say, "The only appropriate thing to do is worship."

And as we sang, we felt the mixture that Christians for thousands of years have felt deep in their veins. Steve's death was what he lived for. He had been swallowed up by life. And as we sat on the worn-out couch where Steve had sat for the last time just a few days before, we knew he was meeting God.

ten

I love when weekends come in gently to the suite I share with my husband, especially the spring ones when we can raise the windows and see the screens we forgot to remove for winter. Usually the first few thoughts of morning cause me to believe it can be a good day, because if the birds outside are happy enough to be twittering, then I should be happy too. The freshness of the sun coming up, ushering in plans that don't involve the office, help move me from pillow to shower to yoga mat.

I pray my way through the weekend mornings, peaceful because I get to watch him sleep as I start my day, no caregiver coming in. I pray my way through because I know I might not love him as much as I want to when he wakes up, and I know he could spend the whole day being too tired to do much. So I know I need to anchor myself down—right here, right now—dig my heels into the floorboards underneath me, and steady myself for the doubts and struggles that are sure to toss themselves toward me before the day's out.

"If I could just always feel this," I say to myself, "if I could always look at him like I just did and say, smiling, 'I don't know how I love you this much,' then every day would be so easy. If I never spoke out of anger toward him because I just want him to be able to work right, I wouldn't feel so suffocated and so needy. If I could only always think right, this marriage would be easy. Why do I insist on making this so hard?"

Taken aback at myself, I watch his chest moving slowly toward the ceiling and back.

"Oh my gosh, Ian, how are you so nice?" I've asked him before. I love hearing him say please, and I love hearing him know what he wants and know how to initiate asking for it. There were so many days when he couldn't.

"I have an incredible Savior," he answers me.

There it is, again, that direct and succinct faith in my husband. There it is, the faith I don't have, but the faith I want to absorb. I know that absorbing it means continuing in this life and this marriage that can hardly be considered comfortable. I know it means continuing to enter into the darkness, turning myself over and over into and through the hands of the potter. I know that for some reason I still need this churning, this burning away in my heart, in order to keep going. If I could be given a way out that comes with an easier path, I would only find myself in a worse disposition than if I continue on in the difficulty.

"Isn't this what I have been called to?" I think to myself. This life of dependency on the One who made me? This life that doesn't make me comfortable, because the discomfort is exactly what I need to make heaven more irresistible?

Isn't this what Ian wakes up to every day?

I continue to watch him, his breathing growing deeper and more rhythmic. Sleep engulfs him. The help that God gives . . . it keeps him.

———————

I tried to help Ian remember that his dad was gone, because sometimes it was hard for him to remember. Sometimes his brain decided not to lock the death away but instead set it free, maybe so it wouldn't become real. I tried to walk Ian through it all again, reminding him that the part he did know—the brain cancer—was the part that took him from us. I tried to help Ian grieve, and I sat with him when he cried for his dad. I tried to ask him questions about what he missed the most and what he loved the most.

He dictated something for the blog in November:

> November 10, 2009 (Ian)
> My dad always looked forward to heaven. I'm happy to know that he is there. Now he is experiencing God every single minute of every day. My dad is experiencing health that he never saw here on earth. I miss him, but I know he's happy. It makes me want to try my best with endurance for heaven. I know I'm going to heaven because Christ died. I'm excited for heaven because I'll see God every day. I love the idea of talking to God.

But somewhere in trying to help Ian through the process of dealing with his dad's death, I began to recognize something, and it showed up in my journal letters to Ian. I wasn't letting *myself* grieve.

> *November 20, 2009*
> Since this is a book of letters to you, Ian, I may say that the most grievous part of your dad's death is your inability to remember. And I don't know why

God would allow you to continue to forget, but He has. I'm not God. But how is that mercy? I pray and pray that you would remember and be able to grieve appropriately.

I cannot know God fully. My finite mind tries to compartmentalize and categorize God. My mind also is blocked by my grief and weariness. But this is walking in grace, love. For we were so utterly burdened beyond our strength that we felt we had received the sentence of death.

That's where my heart stops, love.

I miss you.

Love, Me.

I kept moving forward for Ian. Ian kept moving forward for me. His therapists thought he regressed after his dad died. But we, his family, saw more. He was initiating more, and he was showing me affection more. But I was still aching.

November 21, 2009

I'm sad. And anxiousness feels not far off. Maybe this is normal for the amount of grief that we have suffered. God, please be not far off. God, please help me to hold fast. Ian, I'm scared of what I do not know, for heaven would be a wondrous destination. But I fear we may walk through hell to get there.

Love, I fear that I cannot make it through a life together physically. I feel so weary now. And I fear that I may have reached the depths of despair. And how I need to separate my feelings for you and my mental status—I know I love you, but am afraid of losing enjoyment of you as I lose enjoyment of everything else in life.

Tonight as you were working on eating dinner by yourself, you threw down your fork. I asked what you were thinking and you said, "I wish that this was easier." How that broke my heart. I don't understand this. It doesn't make sense. I don't know what mercy always looks like. And I don't know why you were chosen for this suffering. Oh, Ian, I want you to get to heaven soon. I can't imagine life without you, but you would be so happy.

I can't imagine another day like this.

I love you deeply.

I guess it just took me a long time to see—and only in retrospect did I see it—that Steve had kept Ian alive for me by the way he helped me before Ian could. He possessed memories of Ian falling in love with me that no one else harbored. In his makeup were movements and motions that Ian couldn't make anymore.

When I lost Steve, I lost part of Ian.

Yet when he left, it also seemed as though Ian came. Ian was helping me again, in the way that he used to. And although in fewer words, he was showing me truth, like Steve had. In a sense, their roles flip-flopped.

When Ian was gone, Steve was nearby.

When Steve left, God gave me my Ian back.

When the gaps were created, God filled them.

We decided to go away for Christmas that year, because somehow it sounded easier to be far away than in our own home without Steve. Someone lent us their condo at a ski resort, and we made our way to the mountains on a snowy, December day. We piled into the condo and ran around

excitedly, distracted by the chance to sleep in and eat break-
fasts that the boys were required to make as a contribution
for skiing on the slopes. The younger boys decided soon after
we arrived that we needed to make that night Christmas Eve
because they couldn't bear the thought of waiting.

"Do you and Ian want some time alone?" Mary asked.
We never had time alone when we were all together, and
the question made me suspicious. Still, we found ourselves
together on the couch, the Santas on the feet of my adult-
sized footie pajamas tucked under Ian's legs. I knew something was going on, as everyone bolted upstairs to leave us
alone but pretended to act normal.

Awkward conversation started. The moment felt forced.
And then the moment changed, as I noticed something start
to lower from the balcony above. Looking up, I saw a piece
of string tied to a jewelry-sized box, lowering until within
reach.

"Ian, what is that?"

"A ring."

"What kind of ring?"

"*The* ring," he said.

I reached for it and helped him take it out of the box.

There were times, back when Ian was trapped inside the
white walls of a hospital, when my mind would disobedi-
ently travel to the "what-ifs" and "I wonders." I remember,
for example, trying to imagine how he would've proposed
to me, how his mind would've planned it before his brain
had to work too hard. For a man who once jokingly told his
pastor that once he was married, he expected fireworks to
be set off every time he got home from work, an ordinary
proposal simply wouldn't do.

Maybe he would somehow sneak it into a screenplay he
was working on, and then ask me to proofread the script.

When I came upon the character's words, "Will you marry me?" he'd somehow blend himself into those words and bring the Epson Inkjet printed words to life.

Or maybe he would have taken me into the city on a date, a familiar car ride in which we always found the jazz station for the moment when we saw the skyline. A mile or so out of the tunnel, we would round a slight bend in the road to see the city pop out from behind the trees. Jazz—in particular Mr. Sinatra, asking us to go fly with him—would've made the perfect complement. Maybe he would've done it there, in the car, not traditional and on one knee, but perfectly Ian.

Either way, he knew what this moment was, and he knew what he wanted to ask. He had been working with his mom and sister-in-law to choose the perfect ring. Just like the Ian he had been before his accident, he was very particular and specific, and he disagreed with the girls' recommendations. He wanted what he wanted. And that was it.

And here it was.

"Will you marry me?" he asked.

Will you marry me.

He asked.

Soon, six heads popped over the edge of the balcony above, straining to see the newly engaged couple below. Laughing and yelling at them for being so ridiculous, I watched them clamoring down, the girls begging to see how the ring looked that they had worked so hard to find with Ian.

I called and texted and shared and listened as the responses drifted from joy to confusion to questioning. We celebrated that night, and I started to plan our wedding, because I'd been wanting to for so long but was afraid to in my heart. I talked with Jan about what I wanted for the wedding, while I sorted through the zillion thoughts running through my mind that made me jump from fear to amazement to numbness.

The morning after he proposed, as I sat upstairs on the computer looking at wedding sites, Mary found me to tell me that Ian had another seizure while Caleb was helping him out of bed. And then the decorating and invitation ideas didn't matter as much. The thoughts that looked to the future and felt like maybe something could feel normal again drifted into the realization that we still needed medications and hospitals and people around us who knew how to help Ian.

Excitement, yes.

But without reality, no.

The stillness of winter came once we returned back to Warren Road from the cold slopes of the ski condo. The warmth of the new indoor fireplace blanketed my back as I worked on filling our wedding book with ideas and photos of the dress I'd just bought with my mom and sister and with edited versions of our guest list. But we noticed Ian growing tired through the long, western Pennsylvania winter days, and were eventually told by his therapists that he wasn't doing enough, that they wouldn't be able to work with him anymore.

His doctor decided that for her to get to the root of the fatigue, the root of whatever was making him keep his eyes closed all day, he needed to be in the hospital so that she could have full access to him. She also hoped that a few weeks as a patient on the rehab floor would give him the boost he needed. Plus, one of the main goals for her treatment, she said, was to help him be able to speak his vows.

One night in, and we were told the cause of his sleepiness: a buildup of medicine in his body that should have been monitored better. It required just a quick fix, and then Ian was back to me, staying someplace temporarily that offered us hope and offered him a new challenge. He ate breakfast with the other patients, mostly grandmas or grandpas with new knees or hips, and his therapists worked with him to self-feed. He worked on walking (which didn't go well) and on initiating when he needed help. Mary and I met with the therapists on a weekly basis, listening as they recounted what Ian was and wasn't doing, what they felt he could eventually do, and what they felt was out of his reach.

"Ian, I just got offered a job," I said to him, standing between his bed and the small window in his room. I had just hung up with a company where I'd interviewed the day that Ian had moved to the rehab floor. An acceptance of the offer would mean provision for us and benefits for me, and an opportunity for us to find a home.

On April 8, a few days after Ian was discharged, we signed our first lease as a soon-to-be married couple, and celebrated with dinner in Pittsburgh.

It was happening.

This was really happening.

"I promise you I'll make sure that Ian is okay," I had told Steve, sitting next to his bed as the cancer was winning over his body. I meant that promise. I was not going back on it.

But my weakness and messiness often overshadowed my confidence—confidence in myself, and the confidence I'd been given in God. And as our wedding date grew closer, so did my fears and anxieties. My fears bounced around easily, sometimes landing on the fear that I wasn't fit to be Ian's helper. Then there were times when my fears bounced and landed on the familiar game board square called "doubt," a scary place filled with brain injuries and disabilities and other words that terrified me. I mostly landed on this square when I was with people who didn't understand disabilities and didn't know how to slow their lives down so that Ian could fit. That's when my mind would shift from being Ian's helper to being a caregiver of someone who was severely disabled. And in those times, I started to panic, feeling as though my upcoming marriage were a death sentence.

That turned into anger toward Ian and impatience. That turned my mind into defense mode, thinking everyone was telling me Ian had no value, and that I had to justify, over and over and over, why he was worth marrying.

But Ian—he was steady.

"You're marrying more than a brain injury," he told me after a long talk, seven words that convicted my heart.

"But what if I'm not fit to be your helper," I asked him, my anger and inadequacies seeming too big for me.

Immediately he responded, "No way. You would do anything for me."

I knew that God was bigger than my fears and bigger than Ian's brain injury, but the reality of the new life we were heading into, and the way reality felt on bad brain injury days, suffocated me. Was my gut instinct telling me to not marry Ian? Or was that feeling in my gut my heart's response to choosing a life that would be hard? I didn't want to step into the darkness of a disabled life, the darkness of feeling powerless on my own to love or be loved. But I didn't want to step away from it either, because that meant stepping away from Ian.

May 31, 2010

Ian, you are a good man, and you will love me until the day that I die. Ian, you have done so much for me. There is so much that you still want to be able to do for me.

Oh God, please change my heart. Please teach me this love. Jesus, thank You that Ian keeps me on my knees before You, which is right where I should be.

Ian was learning that God was bigger. A big God is what gave Ian confidence to enter into a marriage without abilities he wanted. It meant trusting that this big God would be his provider, and his wifey's provider.

I started working on preparing our first home, now having a place to tuck my yard sale finds into and around. This first home of ours was perfect, a small ranch hidden in the corner of our landlord's driveway. When we walked through it with the Realtor, it was empty and the smells of the last renter were embedded in the carpets and walls. The front porch sat empty, waiting to be filled with dinner parties and nephews. My girlfriends came over and scrubbed walls and toilets and kitchen cupboards while I was working at my new job, then we came over that night and painted the bedrooms charcoal gray.

I had three bedrooms to fill with things that would calm us and make us feel at home. We had a back bedroom to become an office for Ian and David's company, a spare room that would be Caleb's, and a living room ready for our free couch and piano.

I wanted to create a place where Ian would feel comfortable and feel at home.

I wanted to create a place we would love to come home to and where we could love God in.

I wanted to take from May to August to live by myself in our new home and get it perfectly ready for Ian to join me there when we returned from our honeymoon.

With each day that drew us nearer to August 28, my fears, uncertainties, and faith shifted often. I loved being with him. I loved him. But I kept finding myself back on that square of doubt, terrified of my own weakness and my own tendency for giving up easily on relationships. I think I was just terrified of myself.

Not Ian.

July 24, 2010 (Ian)

It is awesome. It's crazy. Getting married is awesome. Larissa makes marriage awesome. She's perfect for a man. She knows what I need and is willing to give it to me. She helps me with my brain injury.

It is hard to speak sometimes. When I can't speak, it's frustrating. Speaking to each other makes a marriage. Please pray for my speech.

We were going to get married on my aunt and uncle's hill, next to their pond on top of the mountain. It was the same mountain that my mom had grown up on and the same house she had lived in. It was the mountain where she had ridden her horses and run out into the woods to play with her eight siblings, barefoot in homemade hand-me-down dresses. We wanted to get married at the top of that mountain where my dad dropped off my mom after their high school dates and where she left from the morning of her wedding, wearing the dress her mom had made, the one we later used for dress-up.

But about the time that we wanted to get married the gas companies were moving in to my mountains, and they claimed that the land they had leased, right where we hoped to stand, would be filled with bulldozers and pipelines by midsummer.

So we moved the wedding plans three miles east to a small plot of land that my parents and brother had owned for two years. The meadow was guarded on one side by thick woods that were perfect for four-wheeler trails. My dad, still a farmer deep inside, started to prepare the grounds for us, spending the summer mowing and spraying away the pesky bugs and having a pole installed for electricity. A late August summer meant the corn at the top of the hill would be past the knee-high stature of July, and maybe we'd be able to play through the corn that night, like we used to do when we were little.

"Ian, why do you want to marry me?" I was asking regularly, because I was trying to remind myself that getting married was a good idea.

"Because I love you."

"Aren't you scared of marriage with a brain injury?"

Of course not. He was proving to be the strong one, like always, as the days moved closer to our makeshift altar underneath a chandelier that Mary found at a yard sale. It was gold and ugly, so she painted it black for us and replaced the broken dangles with crystals that would twinkle above us on the twenty-eighth. Ian was always sure of God and the decision we had made, and his faith was exactly what I needed. His surety didn't discount or chide my questions, but instead quieted them because his confidence was so gentle.

We decided that Ian should be comfortable for the wedding, so we found jeans and vests for the guys. We decided, too, that the ceremony should be at 5:00 so the sun wouldn't have an advantage over Ian.

My girls, all seven of them, ordered little tea dresses of different patterns, some made from vintage sheets or bolts of fabric. We looked for boots to wear because we were getting married in a field, and because boots were more "me" than heels. We were given little boots for our ring bearer, Paladin, who had barely made it past fourteen months, and Ayla, not even a year, and Lydia, who was just past six.

We had a Jack and Jill shower in the mountains, and we sat and opened gifts while I wondered what everyone was really thinking. I wondered if everyone meant what they wrote in the cards or if they more likely thought I was crazy, or if they were mad at Ian for stealing away the future they thought I should have. I wondered if they knew how much I longed for Ian to be able to remember who they were after only meeting them once, and how much I wished that our engagement were different. I wondered if they knew it wasn't fun for Ian to be taken care of by his mom because he couldn't do it himself when he traveled, or even when he was at home. I wondered if they knew how fake it all felt because our life wasn't normal and our marriage wouldn't be normal and we really didn't need a set of dishes—we needed God.

Still, somehow running parallel to these fears and grievances was delight in Ian and delight in having a best friend. A best friend who always wanted to be with me. Who didn't speak unkindly to me. A best friend who, when given a context in which he could concentrate, could show me more about God in a few words than a pastor could do in an entire sermon, simply because Ian was living it. I didn't know how I was still in love with a man who lacked as much outwardly as Ian did, but I also didn't know how God still loved me, someone who had nothing to offer Him. Yet both had happened to me—and were happening to me—and were making my life infinitely better.

Because we couldn't understand what would unfold for us in the perfect confines of marriage, we could only anticipate in part. The way we needed to look at marriage then was the way I look at children now.

"I don't know the joy that comes with being a parent," I told our friend Dave. "I can only anticipate the hard things. Like figuring out how I would help Ian with his dinner plus kids. Or how to get up in the middle of the night to take care of a baby and then wake up in the morning and help Ian shower."

"The incredible joys you experience as parents far outweigh the difficulties," Dave said laughing.

Our pastor told us something very similar during a counseling session, sessions where we didn't follow the normal handouts because they were more strictly role-based, roles that would be different for us.

"Your marriage will have much deeper valleys than marriages without a disability," Joe told us as we sat under the sun on Mary's patio. "But because you'll know those valleys, you will experience much higher peaks as well."

I believed him. And I asked God to help my unbelief.

"Look what God has done," a church friend said with tears in her eyes, a friend who had watched and prayed and pleaded from a distance. "Look what God has done!" She was seeing our marriage through eyes I didn't have, eyes that scanned all the way from birth, to lives that intersected, to one step from death and then to this, to marriage. She was seeing all that God had accomplished in us, and she was seeing with greater faith than I could muster up on my own.

The heat of July started drifting into August as we made our way to the lake for two weeks. It was the first vacation without Steve, a vacation where no one would be doing puzzles inside, and we would need to get Ian into the water without his help.

Mary told us we were going to rent a pontoon boat, all of the Murphy kids, and go out onto the lake to spread his ashes. I hadn't even stopped to wonder where they were. I had never wished there was a grave to sit by to remember him, because a grave was not where memories would be. He was found all around the house, like stepping into the garage, his workshop still assembled to the right just inside the door. He had meticulously organized and labeled everything, from extra door and drawer knobs to bolts and screws.

The boys struggled to get Ian onto the boat, the owner eventually telling them to do a fireman's carry on him instead of attempting to get the chair over the wobbly dock and onto the bobbing boat. He had been a caregiver, he told us, and knew how to move "people like that" around.

Once we settled, Ben drove us out onto the lake, the breeze whispering across the boat seats where Steve should've been. I pretended we weren't on a boat to spread ashes, but instead were like every other family on the water that day, enjoying a simple Virginia afternoon.

We reached a remote spot, away from the traffic of water skiers and tubers. I watched as Mary sat with her five children, baby grandson, and Jan and I, holding an urn filled with the one who brought this family into being with her. She stepped to the edge of the boat and removed the lid to show the plastic lining holding all that was left of Steve's physical body. Ashes freckled the topmost layer of water as the urn was turned and emptied.

Soon the lake would swallow and toss Steve into itself, washing him away into its centuries-old folds. There he would remain, his body that served him so well, floating on top of and under the boat and Jet Ski ruts, drifting peacefully along the shores his children loved.

———

Returning home from the lake meant less than a month until the wedding, as I drifted from excitement to just wanting the day to be over. I wanted the decision done and final. The details were my love—scripting handwritten notes to each guest to string on a clothesline, finding the perfect handmade rings for my bridesmaids, collecting belt buckles for the groomsmen, ordering hand fans.

Even though memory wasn't a strength for Ian, he knew that something coming up on August 28 was going to change his life. He connived with Ben and David to plan a honeymoon, a honeymoon that would be a surprise to me until we got in the car on the twenty-ninth and started driving south. I loved that I didn't know, because I knew every other detail, and this was something I didn't have to think about.

Our new home was nearly ready for Ian to move into, our new adjustable bed covered in the new gray sheets from my shower at Gigi's. His dresser was ready, an ugly brown mid-century armoire that I found at a thrift store and painted black to accent our yellow, gray, and black duvet. It was starting to feel like a home as I hung paintings created by our friends on the white living room and hallway walls. Our KitchenAid mixer rested on the marble countertop next to the brown bread box that matched our oven. It was starting to feel really good, the good that means something is comfortable and has become a place of rest.

Because we'd be hosting caregivers in and out of our new home, I wanted our bedroom to be an escape, a place where other people weren't getting into our dresser drawers to get his socks in the morning and a place where we could shut out the noise of the company working in the next bedroom.

> *August 12, 2010*
> 16 DAYS UNTIL OUR WEDDING!
> I can be scared sometimes to get married. I think since our engagement I started putting all of these expectations on you, and instead of just enjoying you, I keep thinking and thinking and thinking about your brain injury.
> Ian, I want to love you better. I want the Holy Spirit to fill me with a tender love for you and an enjoyment of you that passes over your disabilities.

Underlying all of my doubts was one anchor to hold onto: love—my love for Ian that had not changed, and God's love for us that would never change or be exhausted and Ian's love for me. I had asked God to take love away if we weren't meant to get married, because I didn't want to wrong Ian. But Ian's love for me had not changed, and his tenderness just seemed to be growing as his abilities returned.

So I timidly moved forward into a step of faith that was unlike anything else I had ever done. I stepped into marriage knowing I was making a decision based on dependence to God, trusting that surely goodness and mercy would follow.

Ian stepped into marriage having to reconcile his fears with what he knew of God. His fear was of not being able to give the care he would want, but he ended on knowing that God was stronger.

I left for Sullivan County on the Wednesday before the weekend that would host our wedding, to have time with my family and time to make last-minute touches to the wedding. Ian was going to come with his family on Thursday, and we would all spend Thursday and Friday together in the mountains. We wanted a weekend of all truly being together, so we booked every available cabin at a state park near the wedding site, which meant bunk beds and outhouses and flashlights at night. Ian stayed in the accessible cabin and spent all day Friday and Saturday enjoying his groomsmen and saying inappropriate things about what he was looking forward to about marriage.

I stayed ten minutes uphill at my parents' house, due north from the cabins, getting the property ready as my uncle unloaded trailer loads of state fairground benches and picnic tables. We covered the splintered ones with fabric so we wouldn't hurt our guests, and my dad hung that black chandelier from the tree branch. The field was filled with hopes for our wedding day . . . and with hopes that someday our vows of sickness and health would show much more of the latter.

———

It's my husband's last day of twenty-seven, and as the tennis balls thud around the dryer with our down comforter, I hear Devon and Ian reading the Bible. I reminded him earlier tonight that he wouldn't be twenty-seven anymore by tomorrow.

"I hope I still like you when I'm twenty-eight," he said laughing.

He brings me so much delight, I thought to myself as I laughed out loud at him. I can't understand how his brain works so quickly with wit, yet so slowly with things like moving his body. Somehow deep inside his brain are neurons that know exactly what to do with the comments I make. Incredible.

Mary says Ian reminds her of her dad, now that Ian's accident makes him say fewer words. Because when he says fewer words, each one is calculated and quality, usually witty and always worth writing down. That's how her dad was, Ian's Grandpa Berger.

Grandpa Berger was someone Ian would want to be like. He grew up in Chicago, the middle of three children. As a young boy he made a point of riding his bike to the theater where Dillinger had just been captured and killed by the Feds. He wanted to see the blood on the sidewalk, which instantly made him cool to his four Murphy grandsons. Adding to his coolness, he became a weightlifter and lifeguard on Lake Michigan, and a ground-breaking scientist who also wrote prose and poetry as a hobby and had a love for words.

Ian's turning twenty-eight tomorrow, more valuable to me now than at twenty-six. And I wonder how this could possibly be, how love can possibly keep growing, because I know it will.

Before me is a small wicker chair and stool with a Ball jar of hydrangeas, reminding me of our wedding flowers. This spring, I asked Ian if I could always keep fresh flowers in our room, even just one bud, and even if it costs a few dollars.

"If it will make you happy, yes."

Without hesitating, he wants me to be happy, even if that happiness comes in light green stems with legs criss-crossed over each other, floating in the glass jar.

We were sitting at the eight-foot table next to the support beam at the church I grew up in when I realized that I, too, had a brain injury. I realized that getting married in the next eight hours meant understanding someone else's grief in an unexpected way. I realized sitting there next to my bridesmaids at a breakfast my mom had prepared for the bridal party and out-of-town guests that I was about to become disabled. I was approaching two words that would mean the end of a life on my own with a healthy body, and the taking on of Ian's flesh.

But it was right to sink into him and his life as I sat there eating pancakes and strawberries, because it meant I was experiencing something God had reserved for that day, for that moment. In the past four years, I had grieved for myself and my own loss much more than I had grieved for Ian's, and this feeling was about to shift. It *had* to shift, because we were stepping into this together. And from 5:00 p.m. that night until one of us made it to heaven, every step we would take and every loss we would encounter would be done together.

Beginning at 5:00 p.m. that night, I was disabled.

My very last letter written to Ian was on our wedding morning, 8.28.10. It summed up the five years' worth of letters I was preparing to give him as a wedding gift.

August 28, 2010
It's our wedding day. We're actually and truly getting married. I'm scared/happy/thrilled/nervous. You are such a blessing to me. And I get to spend my life with you.

We made it. We did it, love. We're going to be married. In nine hours. Writing this is making it even better.

Love you. Next time I write I'll be your wife.

Love, Me.

A light breeze carried Nick Drake's voice through the speakers and out over the guests waiting on old wooden benches. The men sat next to our pastor, Mark, in their jeans and gray vests. We didn't want everyone to stand because it would be hard for Ian, so we hauled my vintage metal chairs to the field and arranged the mismatched set eight on each side of Mark. We didn't want a wheelchair at the wedding either, so Ian's groomsmen carried him wherever he needed to go.

I waited at the top of the hill with my bridesmaids, the breeze blowing and swishing the golden cornstalks. My dad had attached his trailer to the four-wheeler and pulled all of us the mile from my parents' house to the wedding site, our floral handmade dresses and boots bouncing along the dust of the country roads.

The music shifted from an album to the voices of Ian's brother Caleb and cousins Anastasia and Rebekah. I remembered them practicing this song on vacation, all of us gathered onto the back porch at the top of the grassy hill that nestled the lake. Now, though, it was happening for real, which meant that Eight Twenty Eight had finally come.

From where I stood with my dad, I couldn't see the ceremony. We were tucked up in the woods at the top of the hill that overlooked the tents and benches and chandelier. My bridesmaids started to walk, one after the other, into four years of watching their cousin and best friend and sister fight to hope. They walked into four years of teary-eyed conversations, of feeling guilty that their lives were moving on, and of feeling incapable of taking away our loss. Tears met each of their cheeks as they brushed past the guests and then sat one by one on the pink and orange bridal party chairs.

My dad was standing with me at the top of the hill, and he held my hand as the breeze rustled in from the south, reminding me that Steve was there somewhere. He held my hand as we stepped down the hill toward our families and friends and toward Ian. Dad squeezed my hand and fought back tears as we caught sight of him, standing there with the help of his best friend. I felt myself slipping into tears as I walked, but I knew if I gave them enough room, they would be there for hours.

Years had been sacrificed for us to make it to this day, and we lived every one of them under the help of our parents. Their four lives had been completely wrapped up into their children—Ian, their oldest, and me, the Whiteleys' youngest—through infancy and homework and ICUs.

I didn't see it very clearly then, but part of Steve was waiting for me at the altar—his character deposited onto his son in ways that would reveal themselves in the role Ian was stepping into on this perfect summer night. I was getting part of Steve back through the character he had built into his son, and I would soon continue to benefit from him in ways that could only come because of Steve's faithful devotion.

Wrapping his arms around me into a kiss, my dad left me at the altar with a man he knew couldn't take care of me the way my dad wanted him to but hoped this was what his daughter really, truly, wanted.

"This is a trip you will never forget."

Mary was in the kitchen listening to me talk about plans with my dad, plans for a father-daughter trip in Charleston, a city that promised sprawling plantations and tiny cafés. We were taking a birthday trip, since we shared the same special day. He drove to our house, then we drove to the airport. I was scared to leave Ian, because when it came time for the trip, he still wasn't talking yet. My dad promised me an adventure and promised me that we would laugh.

The car rental employee tried to give us a minivan, but we opted for the sports car. Rolling the windows down before the engine was even started, we breathed in the deep southern air that swirled warmly around the coupe. Our northern air hadn't caught up to the seasons of the south, which made the Carolina sky truly warm our lungs, an unfamiliar April guest.

My memory captured a moment with my daddy as he sped down the road covered by a lush canopy of trees. He was testing out the acceleration and testing himself to see if he still had his high school guts. As he drove, I lowered the passenger window, and my hair found its way out, gushing back against the car door. I squealed in delight as my dad laughed, the old country road taking us somewhere unknown but somewhere perfect.

For those few moments in our little blue coupe, I was six again, sitting in the car for the Haunted House at Knoebels Grove, the amusement park where my dad took us every summer. I was bracing myself for the unexpected jumps inside the house and the extra screams my dad would add to scare us.

For those few moments, I was his little girl who had cast her cares.

For those few moments, we lived together in the freedom of forgetfulness.

———————

The sun set perfectly over our heads as the wedding ceremony moved onward. I shared my vows with Ian, and I didn't say "in sickness and in health," because that was the line that made me cry at every other wedding. It made me cry because I didn't know what the second part meant . . . but I did know sickness.

Ian repeated his vows after our pastor, his speech still rough and hard to understand. I knew what he was saying. And David knew what he was saying, since he'd been practicing the vows with him for weeks. He could even be seen mouthing the vows as Ian spoke them. (We would later joke that I had accidentally married *both* of those men that night.)

"I love you," I whispered into Ian's ear after this part of the ceremony had ended and the guests began to stand. There was no walking out and down the aisle together, so our guests came to us. Mary met us as we sat on the chairs, and snuck Ian the wedding present he had bought for me: a jewelry box that gently held a small, silver necklace. I hadn't worn a necklace that morning, maybe subconsciously.

The crowd of our dear ones drifted into us, giving us hugs and best wishes and tears. We sat on the metal rocker I had spray-painted red and white underneath the wall of trees. Our families shifted in and out, around us and beside us, as the moment was frozen onto the screen of a camera. The boys carried Ian in a chair to the break in the woods where we each sat in white leather chairs, hands and lips together in a moment of celebration.

The reception was made perfect by the hard work of my mom—ordering the classic end-of-summer meal: corn on the cob, pulled pork, baked beans, and salad. Our friends made their way to the homemade photo booth and listened as our musicians sang again for us. The dance party erupted and we filled the tent, creating a blur in my mind that's even now pieced together with smiles and laughter and lights dangling from the tent edge.

Once the darkness of night settled in and our ice cream and Oreos were served, we were told to step outside of the tent for a surprise.

Ian and I moved to the open air and watched the sky, waiting. Soon overtop our heads began to rise lanterns, lanterns that filled and expanded into the night air. Ian held my hand as we looked up into the big black of a country sky, each lantern drifting up into the unknown, each lantern having been set on its way by someone we loved.

We kept our necks strained to the sky as they continued to blow upward, creating a new constellation as their flames flickered inside each wax cylinder.

I gasped and smiled and didn't want it to ever end. Ian sat, gazing upward, smiling and laughing. As the lanterns drifted over our heads, we saw love—love that my family shared with us that day, loving us through the details and the beautiful memories they were creating and the surprise they had saved for us. Fifty lanterns floating above us with no other lights to compete against, our wedding site plopped in the midst of forest and cornfields, becoming tiny flickers and specks in the night.

And then—just as we thought we'd seen the last—fireworks began to crackle and explode over our heads. My uncle, hiding up in the cornfield where I had stood earlier with my dad, released giant bursts of hope into the sky as we yelled and cheered.

They did everything to make the night perfect—everything that could be in their control. Much was left undone in our hearts, of course, the longing for healing and the empty table setting where Steve should have been. Yet they filled those gaps with the love they had for us that grew deeper with each loss.

Love has a way of doing that.

We made our way back into the tent with smiles and legs ready to keep dancing, our feet pounding the rented wooden squares that covered the meadow floor. Lydia and I cleared the floor for a sister's song, a Murphy version of the *White Christmas* classic. David and Lisa gave their speeches, filling us with laughter.

The guests started to trickle out, then someone reminded us to cut the cake. The cake that Beth had made that morning in my mom's kitchen passed from our hands to our mouths, and then Ian kissed me.

Soon many of the guests made their way to their cars, but we didn't want to leave, and Mary didn't want to leave. "I'm always ready to leave weddings," she said. "But I want this one to last forever."

Yes, it had all been too perfect. And so calm. The sky was resting perfectly over our tent, and the strands of light cast just enough of themselves to beg us to stay longer.

For six hours, Ian had smiled and laughed. For six hours, Ian had celebrated the joy of becoming a husband, one remarkable purpose for which God created man. Ian and I together had just spent six hours with the best of friends and with the families who had come to show their love, to show that they were with us, walking into this with us.

But we knew that we couldn't hold this moment forever. And so before too long, David drove us to our little cabin by the creek. When I pushed the wooden door open, we saw that someone who loved us had snuck in to light candles. We looked at the atmosphere and looked at the bed and laughed that in four words—"I do, I do"—everything had changed. We entered into our covenant that night and into our new and sovereignly disabled marriage.

———

"Lovey?" I turn toward him to get his attention.

"Yeah?"

"What's the best benefit of being my husband?"

He smiles a dangerous smile, because I know I've set him up for an answer that wouldn't be appropriate for some audiences.

"I'm searching for one answer," he says, stalling.

"Okay, that's the sweetest thing in the world. But honestly, name one."

"One benefit is sex."

"I knew it!" I yelled.

I knew that his answer would involve "the word," and the reason is two-fold—because he lost his discerning social-cue filter in 2006, and because he really loves sex, like I'm told most men do.

"Why is that on your mind so much?" I ask him.

"I'm cursed."

Laughing again because of his efficiency of words to say so much in so few, I gently kiss him and remind him of the slew of reasons why I love being his wifey.

"You encourage me, and you're kind, and you're tender toward me," I utter between small kisses meant to affirm him, letting him know that he holds tremendous value in my heart and takes up a significant amount of space in my head. "You trust me, and you always want to be with me, and you support me . . ."

Talking it through, remunerating them for him out loud, listing off my many reasons for marital gratefulness, stirs something inside of my heart, reminding me what's at the center of my heart in this relationship. Looking at him resting next to me, wrapped inside a thin white microfiber sheet, my affection causes flip-flops in my stomach. He always wants to be with me, always chooses me, always greets me with a big smile and, "Hi, wifey!"

"How was your day?" I'll ask him.

"Better now that my wifey is home."

It's repetitive because I'm a root of gratefulness in his heart . . . daily.

I love being Mrs. Murphy, a name that I don't believe I've actually ever been called out loud in the years we've been married. But it's a name that means I reap the great benefit of being married to a good man.

"Ian, I feel like I just can't be what I need to be at work anymore."

"The problem is the first three words of your sentence."

There it is again, so quickly and succinctly, reminding me that sometimes my whining is a result of feelings that aren't worth even a second glance.

I love being Mrs. Murphy because it's a title I had longed to bear, a title that means we hold each other's hearts. It's a title that means the years of confused dating, the years after we met and the years after the station wagon crunched, have all culminated into a commitment with my best friend, my confidant.

"Ian, I was tempted to lust tonight, after an able-bodied man."

"What can I do to help you?"

"Why aren't you taking this personally?" I asked, bewildered because if the roles were reversed, *I* would certainly take it personally.

"Because it's a holy God you're up against," he answers.

Later when I repeated the story to someone, they were caught off guard that I would be so open with Ian. That we would share this much honesty. But it just makes sense to me, because I've always told him everything, whether we were sitting in his Mazda outside my house or I was sitting next to his hospital bed as the IV dripped fluid into his veins. I tell him everything because I trust him. And I know if he messes up, or if he says something to me that doesn't line up with the Bible, he can trust me to help him get back on track.

It's a pleasure to be married to a good man, a man so much like his dad.

"Ian, my grandma is giving us her car!" I exclaimed after ending the call with her where she verbally shared her gift. "Now we can do something with *our* car. Can we sell it and put the money toward a house?" I asked, knowing we shouldn't but sorely being drawn toward the savings we could have.

"No, we need to give it away, too."

Again he caught me, and he steered me, and he led me into generosity, which meant making the best phone call ever to Ben and Jan, whose own car had just died.

It's delightful being married to a man who makes me so much better.

And who makes me laugh . . .

"Ian, I think I need to sell my soul to writing this week."

"Just make sure you get a good price, preferably $49.99."

Like the days in the hospital and the long, wearying days on Warren Road before we knew marriage, God lets Ian show me exactly what I need, perfectly timed.

Too quickly after our marriage, I forgot how much better it was to be married than to be dating. I forgot what it felt like to see the bedroom door closed and hearing the voice from inside. Marriage, this marriage, has let me come to know Ian. It has let me experience him in a way that I couldn't before. There is now no place I cannot go, in his mind and in every corner of his heart. I can now learn to know him fully, and experience him fully, without restraint or fear—because God has given him to me and I to him. And he shares in those same joys.

I've become his helper in a way I didn't know before. For the first time on our honeymoon I could do what I had never done before, could become to him what was restricted before. Overnight those servings, that laying down of myself, became the veins through which God poured the most heartfelt gratitude and joy. In those tunnels that were being carved with each pill container I filled and each catheter bag I emptied into the toilet was beginning to trickle a small stream that connected me to God's heart, a stream that over years of experiencing the gift of being someone's helper would build into a stronger current, eventually bursting through the walls that had held it in, tumbling and spilling over, grace tumbling over grace.

"You've been happier since you got married," my mom said, just a month before the day that would mark three years.

Yes, God has given us a mystery in each other that we will unpack and uncover each year that we have together. He has given me an irreplaceable gift through my disabled husband who in few words has helped me more than any—more than can be told.

"Ian, what would you say to people who tell Larissa she shouldn't have married you?" he was asked once during an interview. We had told them (the ones who were conducting the interview) stories about the hurtful comments we receive, the judgment, the criticism.

"They should spend a day in Larissa's life," Ian said.

"Why?"

"Because they would see that she has a husband who loves her."

The simple beauty of this marriage is the truth he speaks and the God he loves. We live as two empty vessels, vessels that we know not how to fill on our own, but are completed and perfected through what we receive down, what trickles down, from perfect love in Him.

"Ian, I did five laps last time. Remember what goal you set for me for today?"

"Increase by half."

"And I did!"

"I'm so blessed to be married to you," he says, turning his head to the right to see my dripping wet swimsuit.

"Why?" I ask.

"I'm so lucky!"

"Why?"

"Because you know how to push yourself."

With each stroke and lap I had been thinking of him, thinking of how proud, how happy he would be that I kept going, didn't give up. Because that's how he lived his life. I wanted to tell him that I was doing it, that I was accomplishing the double goal he had set for me. I was excited because I knew when I returned to the blue lounge chair where he rested, I would be treated with encouragement and tenderness.

"I love you. Thank you for always encouraging me," I say to him, after moving to his left side and standing above where he's lying.

"Thank you for being thankful."

"Oh stop it!"

"I did."

Laughter, then silence.

The wind shifts the leftover water droplets from my hair onto the lenses of my pink thrift store grandma sunglasses, and the towel resting on my shoulders gently flaps the back of my thighs. I feel a tug on the right corner, and looking down I see his wedding ring hand clasping the terry cloth as I stand over him.

"That towel looks really good right now."

"Ian, you're obsessed with towels!" He's always asking for them, always at the same time, like after he finishes brushing his teeth or as soon as he gets in the pool to swim.

A smirk and the pause of his thinking that usually means sass will soon appear. "You're waiting for me to respond with something smart," he says.

"Yeah. So?"

"So, it's not comin'," he says.

"Why not?"

"Because I want a towel more."

I just stand and look at him, smiling, because I forget how much fun he is. He's just getting over an infection that wipes him out and hides his humor, taking his smiles and his progress from me. They're common visitors to his body and should not surprise me or set me back as far as they do. But when he's not well, I don't do well. Since I've been with him tonight, though, just half an hour since leaving work, I've enjoyed every minute with him. I haven't been thinking about his brain injury or wishing he could just walk into the water himself instead of me needing to help him. I haven't been angry at him for not asking me more questions about my day or drawing me out in any type of conversation. I've just been focused on him, and on the ways he makes me laugh, and on how perfectly handsome he looks four days past a good shave.

And that feeling, that feeling of just enjoying someone and delighting in them, is so freeing, so refreshing, so welcomed—because the opposite of it makes me feel like I'm dying. And that's not a place I want to be. Because in that place, the future is terrifying, even though it's a place of terror and hopelessness that sometimes feels necessary to show me that I'm not the one who holds my marriage. The days of darkness and depths of valleys make the relief of God much stronger and the desire for final relief much greater.

The days of looking at what we want and seeing that we cannot get there need to happen, I suppose, because without them we may love this place a little too much.

I wouldn't know what it's like for that gap to be breached. For without the hard places, I would not recognize my lack or the sweeping presence of God.

In this place, where I look at Ian and see God and the cost Jesus paid so that we could know and experience love, we see clearly that He does work all things—together.

epilogue

July 25, 2013 (Ian)

My time here is great. I've been swimming today for hours. Sarah and Jessie are here, and Larissa.

I feel so free sitting here because my wifey is sitting on my lap. The sound of the waves is repeating into my brain. The breeze rushing over me is a wonderful feeling. The dock is kind of like how I feel—it envelops me just like my family that envelops me. They're everywhere and they ask me how I'm doing. I go up to the house and my grandma is there to greet me.

This lake brings back so many memories, like sunburns on my back and seaweed shrinking onto my hands. I used to spend hours swimming with the seaweed and lying on my back in the shallow end looking at the stars. My cousins would play football in the yard and cards on the tiki bar, their voices echoing all over the house.

Grandma Berger would always make bread, and Grandpa would swim laps in his short 1960s trunks.

Uncle Eric was always working on the boat, taking kids out tubing and at night going fishing.

I've always smiled when I think about the lake because it's my happy place. At the lake, all my cousins are there and they love being there. Everybody's happy. My favorite thing to do at the lake is hang out with my cousins doing whatever. Sarah and I like to hang out in her room talking about our lives.

I see God in all my cousins' smiling faces, because He is happiness.

I know what Ian means—because I haven't been this happy since last year when I was at the lake. Something happens when I'm here with Ian's family—all thirty-eight of us this year—when we walk into the tiki house that sits on the edge of the lake. Something is pushed out of me, a tightness that hides in me, tucks away in me when I'm not here by the water.

This year has been the best, because Ian is doing the best. He walked up all the steps to the tiki bar for the first time since 2006, and he sat in the tall barstool chair overlooking the docks as the sun set. We posed for replica luau photos and wondered if the phone was capturing the true colors or just distorting them. He got in and out of the boat more easily, because he's getting stronger. We didn't need to take a ramp to get into the house, because he could walk up the stairs instead.

These two weeks on the lake or on the bay in New York have forged lives together and have enveloped me into them. Grandma and Grandpa Berger have watched as their

children and grandchildren and great grandchildren have
gathered in the summer when they can, making their way
back into each other's lives after months apart. For years and
generations, God has been faithful to these families. And we
all share in the blessing.

At the lake is healing, because we are all together and we
are loved, despite the messiness of the past twelve months.
Inside that little cocoon, we rest—and Ian rests—because in
this cocoon, no one is telling him that he has no value, and
no one is telling me that I shouldn't have married someone
with no value.

Inside the cocoon of the lake, we're wrapped into each
other's memories, and wrapped into people who have known
Ian his entire life.

It feels safe.

It feels like home.

It feels like maybe it's a sprinkling of heaven on our taste
buds, whetting our appetites for the home we will never
have to leave. It feels like a foretaste of redemption.

It's like his cousin Sarah's dream, the one she recalled
having a few days after leaving. In her dream, Ian was walking down a long, twisted staircase to meet her and me at
the bottom. It took him so long, and it took so much work,
trying to maneuver without his cane, making the steps even
more arduous.

Then, just as he was alighting from the last step—his
dad appeared—bounding down the stairs behind him,
laughing boisterously, filled with pride because his son was
growing so strong, just as he knew he would, just as he had
fought and advocated so tenaciously for. In her dream, Steve
had never died, had never disappeared. He had simply been
there waiting for us all along, only whole and healthy and
radiant, receiving perfectly all that he had ever lacked on

earth, appearing closer to Christ's image than our eyes had ever consumed. He opened us into him and wrapped himself around his son from whom earth had separated him, sweeping him up into infinite love and delight.

Sarah embraced her uncle.

"We've missed you," she gasped.

"Oh, I love you all more than you could ever know."

All had been restored. All had been redeemed. Brokenness had disappeared into light.

June 25, 2008 (Steve)

I see God in the way that Larissa has stayed with Ian through this. I don't know the future; I don't know what the Lord has for her. I wouldn't be at all bitter if she decided it was time to move on. I wouldn't at all begrudge her that course of action. But, right now, I see the Savior in her devotion. I know she's a sinful person created by God like me, and I know she's limited in her capacity for devotion . . . unlike God. Yet God allows her to reflect Himself through her care and devotion for Ian.

God is limitless in His capacity to remain devoted to me, though I don't deserve His care. I sin against Him time and time again day after day, but the Bible says that His mercy never comes to an end. Even if I had never sinned against Him, compared to God's infinite nature we're nothing that He should consider a treasure. Yet, that's exactly what the Bible says about those who have offered their feeble, limited devotion to Him. "What is man that you are mindful of him or the son of man that you care for him?"

Larissa's devotion directs my attention to the Savior. It is a glimpse of Christ. If in saying this, I've caused your mind to dwell on her devotion, I've messed up. If in any of our posts we have directed attention to ourselves, we have messed up. When we see Larissa and Ian together, we should not be amazed by her devotion and love. Instead we should be pointed to Christ, amazed by His love for us and the miracle it is that we can reflect even a portion of that. Please don't insert comments in response to this post with high praises for her because this is not about her or myself or my family. It is a picture of Christ's devotion to me. Christ's devotion to me as I reflect on it from the vantage point of heaven will no doubt take my breath away. I don't deserve it, but I'm amazed by it.

Thank You, Lord!